The Bookseller's Art: Carl Kroch and Kroch's & Brentano's

The Bookseller's Art: **Carl Kroch and Kroch's & Brentano's**

A publication of
The Center for the Book
in the Library of Congress
in association with the
Illinois Center for the Book

*Kroch's & Brentano's on Wabash: a
landmark location for several generations
of Chicago's readers. Photo by Bill
Hedrich, Hedrich-Blessing.*

The Bookseller's Art: **Carl Kroch and Kroch's & Brentano's**

Edited by
John Y. Cole
Director, The Center for the Book

Library of Congress
Washington, D.C.
1988

To write books is easy,
it requires only pen and ink
and the ever patient paper.

To print books is a little more difficult,
because genius so often rejoices
in illegible handwriting.

To read books is more difficult still,
because of the tendency to go to sleep.

But the most difficult task of all
that a mortal man can embark on
is to sell a book.

Sir Stanley Unwin
1848–1935

This book is printed on permanent/durable paper

Library of Congress Cataloging-in-Publication Data

The Bookseller's Art

    1. Kroch, Carl. 2. Kroch's & Brentano's. 3. Booksellers and bookselling—Illinois—Chicago—History—20th century. 4. Booksellers and bookselling—United States—Biography. 5. Chicago (Ill.)—Intellectual life—20th century. I. Cole, John Young, 1940–
Z473.K94B66 1988   070.5'092'2 [B]   88–600439
ISBN 0–8444–0624–4 (alk. paper)

Front cover: Carl Kroch in his favorite
room perusing a favored book, 1984.
© Chicago Tribune, 1988, world rights
reserved.

Contents

Preface

Booksellers have helped shape American life and letters since colonial days. A mediators between those who create books and those who buy and read them, they perform an important educational and cultural function. This role is, however, becoming a difficult one for a bookseller to play, largely because of increasing competitiveness in the book industry. Economic pressures have quickened the bookseller's traditional dilemma: how to pay homage to the book and serve the community while still making a profit?

In this century few booksellers have solved this dilemma as successfully as Carl Kroch and his father Adolph, and few bookstores have been as important to the cultural life to their community as Kroch's & Brentano's of Chicago. Historian John Tebbel once described bookselling as "a marrying of minds, not only through the ideas and emotions that books convey to readers and sellers, but among all those literate people who make, sell, and buy books." The Kroch family booksellers have stimulated the "marrying of minds" in Chicago for over 80 years.

The Center for the Book in the Library of Congress, established in 1977 to enhance appreciation of the importance of books and reading in our national life, is pleased to honor Carl Kroch and the bookselling tradition he and his father exemplify. It is especially appropriate that this publication be a cooperative venture between the Center and its affiliate, the Illinois Center for the Book. Sadly Jeanette Kroch, Carl's wife, died before this volume was published. This appreciation is dedicated to her memory, as well as to Carl Kroch and the unique family also known as Kroch's & Brentano's.

The projects of The Center for the Book and its 17 state affiliates are funded by tax-deductible contributions from individuals and corporations. On behalf of both the Library of Congress and the Illinois Center for the Book, I would like to thank Chas. Levy Co. for a contribution which made this volume possible. Special thanks also go to novelist Irving Stone and publisher Samuel Vaughan for their essays and, for advice and help, to Evelyn Sinclair of the Library of Congress's Publishing Office and to Rhonda Taira of Ligature, Inc. in Chicago.

John Y. Cole
Director, The Center for the Book
Library of Congress

Foreword

The Illinois Center for the Book is extremely pleased at the part it has played in the making of *The Bookseller's Art*. Our concerns as an organization are very well served by this acknowledgement of the crucial part the book store plays in the community of letters and the clear sense that a great book store is a major cultural resource. Also, Carl Kroch helped found the Illinois Center and remains an active member of its Board of directors, and his enthusiasm for Center for the Book activities, both locally and nationally, has been sustaining and infectious.

Promoting books and reading is, of course, the bookseller's business, and no one has conducted it any better than Carl Kroch. His work with the Illinois Center reminds us, though, that the heart of his enterprise has always been a true affection for books and an excitement about reading. Hearing him talk about his own reading or about the importance of encouraging an interest in books in young people, it seems natural to see Kroch's & Brentano's with its great variety and its commitment to customer service as the successful but quite logical extension of the personality of an avid reader. Like its avid reader, the store suggests a general faith in the efficacy of books—their utility for every part of the practical life and their diverse and essential place in the life of the mind, their ability to instruct, delight or transport us.

Michael Anania
President
Illinois Center for the Book

Section I

A Tribute at the Library of Congress
October 27, 1986

*Carl and Jeanette Kroch with Librarian of
Congress Daniel J. Boorstin at the Library of
Congress, October 27, 1986.*

Introduction

Twenty-two friends of Chicago bookseller Carl Kroch paid tribute to Mr. Kroch and the contribution he has made to the world of books at a lunch– eon at the Library of Congress on October 27, 1986. Hosted by Librarian of Congress Daniel J. Boorstin, the event was sponsored by The Center for the Book in the Library of Congress as part of its program to celebrate and document American book culture.

In his opening remarks, Librarian Boorstin emphasized the unique role that Carl Kroch and his bookstore, Kroch's & Brentano's, have played and continue to play in the Midwest. Since 1907 when Adolph Kroch, Carl's father, opened a bookstore in Chicago's Loop, the Kroch family has symbolized bookselling at its best. Carl joined the firm in 1935, a few months after graduating from Cornell University, and became president in 1952 when his father retired. As one of America's leading independent bookstores, Kroch's & Brentano's has had an enormous influence on the entire book trade. Its innovative promotion methods, wide-ranging stock of books on all subjects, and high standards of personal service are known throughout the industry. Mr. Boorstin, however, felt that Kroch's & Brentano's influence as a cultural institution has been at least as impor- tant as its impressive accomplishments as a business. Kroch's & Brentano's encouragement of authors, both local and national, and its enthusiastic support of literary and book activities of all kinds have helped make Chicago an important literary center. Kroch's & Brentano's survival and prosperity demonstrates "how a good bookstore can support, nurture, and enhance the intellectual life, not only of one city, but of civilization itself."

Mr. Boorstin also acknowledged Carl Kroch's loyalty to his customers and staff, his personal enthusiasm for books, and his generosity in sharing that enthusiasm with others. He has been a loyal supporter of The Center for the Book in the Library of Con- gress and of its affiliate, the Illinois Center for the Book, which was established in 1985. In 1982 he made a substantial and innovative contribu- tion to Cornell University, his alma mater, by endowing a chair for the university librarian—one of few such chairs in the United States. Of special significance was Mr. Kroch's recent and "wholly admirable" decision to turn over the ownership of Kroch's & Brentano's to its seven hundred employees.

Before asking those present at the luncheon for recollections and com- ments, the Librarian registered his agreement with Alfred Knopf, Jr., who feels Carl Kroch is "the giant of book- selling in the twentieth century." It was fitting, Mr. Boorstin concluded, that Carl Kroch and the tradition of independent bookselling so well represented by Kroch's & Brentano's be honored by the Library of Congress, the national library of a great free republic which was founded on books and reading.

The recollections and comments that follow were presented at the luncheon or sent to The Center for the Book by admirers of Carl Kroch who could not be present.

William Rickman of Kroch's & Brentano's; George Braziller; Carl Kroch; Librarian of Congress Daniel J. Boorstin; and G. Roysce Smith.

The Kroch Family Booksellers

Irving Stone

The art of bookselling, as exemplified by "Papa" and Carl Kroch, began a full century ago. This is how it all began, as Papa Kroch related the story to me in Chicago in 1934:

> When I was sixteen years old in Lemberg, Germany, I campaigned for the socialist candidate for mayor of the city. He was of course roundly defeated. My father said to me, "You see, you've been a damn fool." No one could call me a damn fool, not even my own father. I gathered up the rare books and first editions I had acquired, and took them to a secondhand bookstore. The owner paid me enough money for my steamship fare to the United States. Since I had only modest English, I went to work in a German bookstore in Milwaukee at a minuscular salary. My first customer asked me for an inexpensive German dictionary. I showed him one that cost two dollars. I then showed him how incomplete this inexpensive edition was, and brought out a twenty-five-dollar German-English edition which was authentic and complete. I said to him, "This dictionary will last you a lifetime and will be used by your children."

The customer bought the twenty-five-dollar edition. The bookstore owner was so staggered by this feat that he increased Papa Kroch's salary and promoted him during his first day on the job.

That was the "Art of Book Selling" in its infancy; and it has flowered to the benefit of all book-lovers and book-buyers through two full and active generations.

In February of 1934, after the page proofs of *Lust for Life* had been sent out, the traveler for Longman Green entered Kroch's Bookstore on Michigan Avenue in Chicago tremulously. He desperately needed an order, but he had figured in advance that Papa Kroch would order one-half a copy of *Lust for Life*, as was the custom in those deep Depression days. Papa Kroch was at his desk, about three-fifth's of the way down the store, dealing with the traveler from another publishing house when he looked up and saw the Longman Green man approaching him. Papa Kroch cried out: "I'll take five hundred copies of *Lust for Life*."

The Longman Green man told me he almost fainted, but saved himself by realizing that Papa Kroch was pulling his leg. Papa Kroch was serious, and gave the man his order. The

Longman Green salesman informed Mr. Mills, the owner of the branch of the old and sacrosanct house in London, of this order. Mr. Mills, who was on board ship going to Europe, cabled Papa Kroch just one word: "Why?"

Papa Kroch cabled back: "Why don't you read the book?"

For the first time that we know of in American bookselling, Papa Kroch took out full-page ads in the Chicago newspapers with his recommendation of *Lust for Life*, which then sold at $2.50, and guaranteed to return a five-dollar bill to anyone who brought the book back, dissatisfied. I asked Papa Kroch how many returns he got.

"One. And I sold a good many thousands."

Those were the days before widespread airplane travel. My wife Jean and I, and one and then two of our children, would take the Santa Fe to Chicago where we were supposed to catch the connecting train for New York with our new manuscript for Doubleday. However, we always stopped overnight at the Kroch home where we were welcomed as part of the family. Carl was then about thirteen, I believe, and Gretchen a year or two older. Gertrude Kroch gave wonderful dinner parties for us, inviting as many of the Chicago writers and book reviewers as she could gather up, including Sterling North, literary editor for the *Chicago Daily News* and Emmett Dedmon, book editor for the *Chicago Sun-Times*. On one of these stay-overs, Papa Kroch said to me after a late party: "Come with me down to the bookstore at eight in the morning. I want to show you something."

We drove to Kroch's Bookstore where Papa took me up to his entresol. There, laid out on two or three rough "horses" was a large and random collection of manuscripts, briefs, correspondence, and the like. Papa Kroch directed me to the rough-hewn tables and said: "This is for you."

I asked, "What is it?"

He replied, "The entire Clarence Darrow literary estate. I bought it from Ruby Darrow a few weeks ago."

I asked, "Why did you buy this, Papa?"

He replied, "It's for you. You're going to write the biography of Clarence Darrow."

I had long revered Darrow as one of our great national heroes and had followed him closely through his trials, such as the Loeb-Leopold case in Chicago and the Scopes evolution case in Dayton, Tennessee. However I had no intention of writing a biography about him. Papa Kroch said: "We'll just keep the papers here until you're ready."

After I delivered my new manuscript and returned home, I tried to write a fictional novel, for which I have no talent whatever. When I saw the new manuscript being unfulfilled, my mind turned more and more to the Clarence Darrow story. One day I called Papa Kroch and asked: "Do you still have that Darrow literary estate on your entresol?"

He replied, "Of course. It stays here until you come and claim it and write his biography."

I went to Chicago the next day and gathered up the Clarence Darrow papers, then laid them out on the same kind of crossed-timbered 'horses' in my own living room in Encino, California. We had just moved into our new home but had run out of money for the furnishings. There was an empty living room just waiting for the Darrow literary estate.

Papa Kroch was indeed the godfather of *Clarence Darrow for the Defense*, which Doubleday is now republishing, with a new and interpretative introduction on the value of Clarence Darrow in American society, to celebrate the fiftieth anniversary of the original publication.

As we wrote succeeding books Jean and I and our children stayed with the Krochs, and I became better acquainted with Carl as he went through high school. He told me at that time that he was not sure he wanted to go into the book business; that he might want to become an engineer. If memory serves me, Carl graduated from Cornell shortly before World War II, and he served as an officer in the U.S. Navy. The war matured Carl, as it did all of our participants. When it was ended he had developed a strong interest and excitement about the book business.

During the following years, whenever Jean and I went into Chicago at the publication of a new book, Carl was always at the airport (there were planes by now) with the Doubleday representative to meet us. That night, or the following night, Carl and Jean-

ette would give us a publication celebration party at the Tavern Club. There again, as we had in the Kroch home on Lake Shore Drive, we would meet Chicago's school of writers and literary critics. At one of these parties Carl sat me next to Eunice Shriver, whose husband, Sargent Shriver, organizer of the Peace Corps, was then head of the Chicago Furniture Mart. She told me the following story: "I was in the hospital in Chicago. My brother Bobby called from Washington to ask how I was. I replied, 'I'm bored.' Bobby said, 'I'm putting a book into the airmail for you. Read it and you won't be bored anymore. It's called *The President's Lady*, about Rachel and Andrew Jackson. But don't read it all in a gulp. Make it last for a couple of days.'"

Through Carl I thus met the Kennedy family, and later formed a strong friendship with Bobby Kennedy, who was instrumental in sending Jean and me on the Cultural Exchange to the Soviet Union, Poland, Czechoslovakia, Yugoslavia, and Hungary. Eunice Shriver later brought me her mother's copy of *The Agony and the Ecstasy*, which Rose Kennedy not only had annotated in the margins, but had pertinent maps and helped us chart our route through the Abraham Lincoln country, down to Mary Todd's Lexington, Kentucky.

When Papa and Gertrude Kroch decided to retire and leave the Kroch bookstores to Carl, they chose Southern California. My wife Jean found them a lovely home in Laguna Beach, with a couple of acres of avocados. The Krochs added a beautiful master bedroom and baths; and for many years thereafter we visited them, sometimes with our children. When my son Kenneth was born, Papa Kroch became his godfather.

Carl is inventive and creative in his bookselling. He saw that the only monthly publication telling about the new books being published was a small and not terribly attractive booklet. He designed a beautiful new brochure and asked if I would write the first article for it on the value of books. Of course I was glad to do so.

Papa Kroch read very widely among the newly arrived books, so that he would know what he was selling. Every Friday morning at eight o'clock he gathered together his sales force, reviewing the new publications for them so they would know which books should go to which customers.

Carl, following the family tradition, keeps an intimate contact with the publishers and knows a good many of our American writers. The Kroch bookstores are among our best in the Midwest for their enormous collection. The last time Jean and I were in Chicago, in 1985 with the publication of *Depths of Glory*, Carl and Jeanette gave us a luncheon at the same Tavern Club. He informed me that Kroch's stores now have in stock some two hundred thousand titles. This makes them almost a reference library for a book-buyer who, ardently or desperately needing a title, can have it found on Carl's computer and the

book put into his or her hands quite readily. This is a blessing.

For years I had heard from Carl and Jeanette that they might leave the Kroch bookstores to their employees. I never really believed that the miracle would happen. Now I know that they are very much in earnest, for I have seen a public announcement that Carl and Jeanette have made this marvelous gift to the men and women who have served them and the bookstores so faithfully over the years.

It was a generous thing for Carl and Jeanette to have done. We are all grateful to them. Papa and Gertrude Kroch would have been proud.

A Recollection

Samuel Vaughan
senior vice president, Random House, Inc.
formerly editor-in-chief, Doubleday

In 1954, at the age of twenty-six, I was promoted to be advertising manager at Doubleday and assigned to work with a dynamic, tempestuous, frequently brilliant sales manager named Fred Murray. He told me that one of the first things we should do together was to go to Chicago and meet the trade.

So we went. Along the way, he gave me a little briefing. The Chicago book trade was dominated by a handful of powerful individuals, he said, and important accounts. These included Marshall Field's; a wholesaler named McClurg, for whom the principal book buyer was a frequently acerbic and alternately sleepy man named Guy Kendall; and Stuart Brent, inspired, opinionated, volatile. The particular pride of Chicago, in Fred's mind, was Kroch's & Brentano's, and he wanted me to see their brand new store on Wabash Avenue in the Loop. He told me that another young man, Carl Kroch, had followed in his father's rather substantial footsteps to run the new bookstore. He told me that book salesmen were put to the test in Chicago. With these large accounts, a salesman put his feet in the flames.

I entered Chicago, then, with some trepidation, indigestion, apprehension, and concern, all brought on by Fred's ominous suggestion that if I didn't make it there, I wouldn't make it anywhere. The hold that these men had on the book world, Fred suggested, would make the hold of Mayor Daley look like benevolent absentee ownership. A mild handshake. You were expected to hold your own, to match your weight in martinis or in bourbon whiskey. Martinis? You weren't supposed to count them—the cost or the consequences. For the only time in my life, I wished I were going to Indianapolis instead.

As it happened, Mr. Guy Kendall treated me very kindly. The people at Marshall Field's were rather nice and certainly well-organized. This was the time when downtown, center city department stores counted heavily in retail book sales, pretty much before the invention of the shopping mall, the discounter, and the training academies for muggers and car thieves.

But the people who impressed me most, and who became friends for the rest of my working life—to this day— were people like Wendell Goodpasture, the head buyer for Mr. Kroch; Mort Levin, later to work in publishing at Viking, McGraw-Hill, Avon, and Aperture; and Carl Kroch himself. They could not have been nicer or more helpful. They taught me the astonishments of clear thinking, common sense, regard for the customer, useful skepticism, a practical optimism. They reinforced my belief in the importance of books, their writers, readers, and vendors.

Carl's father had been an inspired and passionate bookseller. Carl was on his way to becoming in his own way an equally inspired and passionate bookseller as well as an innovative one. He was a man who would carefully, thoughtfully, expand a bookstore into a group of bookstores, each with its own character and purpose. Of course there were those from the start who said in effect that Carl would never be the man his father was, or that after the death of his legendary buyer, Wendell Goodpasture, things would go differently—and those remarks, however ill intended, turned out to be accurate. For Carl is not the man his father was; he is very much his own man. And when Goody died, things did go on differently and, in their own way, just fine.

The new Kroch's store was decidedly impressive. You could find your way around it easily and clearly and it was a cheerful place. It had full departments devoted to poetry and to drama. The staff knew what they were talking about and they seemed to care.

We had just introduced at Doubleday a line of what were to be known as trade paperbacks, called Anchor Books, and were paying for racks to be built in Kroch's to accommodate the new rather oddly shaped books.

The legendary buyer, Wendell W. Goodpasture, known as "Goody", who supported Kroch's & Brentano's and Carl Kroch.

But the other remarkable thing is that they were to be put in the basement of the new store. The idea was that customers would be attracted to these books on their new racks. They would be drawn to walk through the entire first floor, past tables of other and more expensive books, and then directed to a brightly lit paperback basement where, wonder of wonders, they were encouraged to pick up a shopping basket and fill it with the new paperback books. The children's room in the back of the store was also meant to be a draw. And they were shortly to create a book catalog for themselves called *Book Chat* and to syndicate it through other booksellers. There were, in general, any number of fresh, innovative bookselling ideas at work in this one place. Despite my loyalty to Doubleday, I thought that Kroch's was then the best general bookstore in the United States, and I still think so.

A couple of years later, when I had become sales manager, I had grown accustomed to the seasonal visits to New York of Carl's buyer, Goody, and his advertising manager, and sometimes Carl himself. We looked forward to these encounters. They were occasionally abrasive and argumentive, but always friendly and always productive.

One year Goody said to me: "Sam, I want to hear about your new books, your list in general, and we want to explain a proposition to you—or at least a dilemma we have." What was that, I asked. Well, Goody said, he knew that we had a fine list of big books for the fall and we would want him to spend quite a lot of his budget on subscribing advance orders for those big books to come. Yes, I said. What's the problem? Well, Goody said that we also had a superb backlist and he know that we would be wanting him to buy the older, established books, the ones that sold year-in, year-out. Yes, I said. What's the problem?

Goody said that the problem is that we want to buy both kinds of books from you but we only have so much money, we can only afford to pay so much at any one time, and we don't want to underbuy. I looked at his rumpled, wise, partly tough and partly amused face, and said, what do you have in mind? I have in mind, he said, that we should buy your backlist books now, early, and have them

shipped into the store in the summer, which would give us time to receive them, unpack them, get them onto the shelves, get our records in order, and so on. And then, buy your new books when your salesman comes to call. Splendid, I said. What am I missing? You are missing, Goody said, my point: I want to buy those backlist books now but I don't want to pay for them until next January.

There was a long pause. About several seasons, I think. I was thinking of the moment not long before when I had become sales manager and my new boss, the white-haired, handsome, and florid-faced Thomas R. Burns, had led me past a row of black, bound looseleaf volumes on the shelf of his office. Do you see those books?, Tom said. Yes, I nodded. Well, Tom said, those are bound volumes of Doubleday testimony before the Federal Trade Commission. They like to examine us from time to time, he explained, because Doubleday not only publishes books, we also print them, sell them at retail, operate book clubs, etc. Whenever the Federals think there might be a case to be made, they prefer to make it against us. So, he said, if you don't want to spend a great deal of time testifying before them and adding to this row of bound, black volumes, keep your nose clean. Remember that you can't make special deals. What you offer one account, you have to offer to all others, for instance.

That memory was with me as I pondered Goody's proposition. Well, Goody, I said, I sympathize. I know what you mean. We would love to do what you have in mind, but I would not love to go to jail: Sure, Goody said, I know what you mean. But think about my problem and see whether there is anything you can do about it.

My boss, Mr. Burns, preferred to get to work at about 7 p.m., roll up his sleeves, and then roll them down at about 10 or 11 p.m. when we would have late suppers at the Drake Hotel nearby. That night I told Tom of my problem. Simple, Tom said, we can't do it. But then as we sat there, the idea slowly emerged, somehow from the synergy of the two of us, plus the Drake's cold beverages, that it might indeed be possible for us to do it for Kroch's and for the rest of the trade.

So we cooked up a little experiment, called, at first, the "deferred payment plan." That first year we wrote orders on backlist books to be delivered in the summer, sold in the fall, and paid for in winter to Kroch's and to a number of other booksellers. The amount was about $600,000, as I recall. Over the years, the volume of that special sale increased into the millions, and much of the rest of the publishing trade followed us.

Later I couldn't tell whether a gun had been put to my head or an inspiration planted there. No matter. It was a case of trying to cooperate with Carl's people and, as in the best of such situations, we all benefitted.

It is fitting and appropriate and a testimony to Carl that he has chosen to make it possible for his employees, his colleagues and co-workers, to become his heirs, for we all have been his beneficiaries in the world of books. Not only an outstanding bookseller but a great book collector and a giver and sparker of causes on behalf of books, Carl, who always gave his employees the best press, has in the end made it possible to give them—or at least sell them—the store. There are many merchants who say "Don't give away the store," but Carl has managed to do that as he did everything else: thoughtfully, patiently, humanely, and we, in the community of the book, are once again all the better for it.

Recollections and Comments

Associates at Kroch's & Brentano's

Ray Carroll
senior vice president,
Kroch's & Brentano's

Kroch's & Brentano's today is a direct reflection of one man's philosophy, personality, and love of books. That man is Carl Kroch. He believes that for every book published, there is someone who is interested in what the author has to say. Someone besides the author's mother, that is. Somewhere there is a customer for every book, from a book on learning how to hang spoons from your nose to a book on the latest breakthrough in computer technology. His philosophy is that people interested in these books should be able to find them in a clean, modern, well-stocked, well-lit, non-intimidating store. The store should be staffed by knowledgeable sales-people with a love of books and a desire to share that love with others. He believes that the customer is the most important person in a business relationship, and that every effort should be made to give the customers what they want. An organization with dissatisfied customers will not survive.

Carl Kroch also believes that people are the most important part of his organization. He backs this up with wage and benefit programs far above industry standards. He also backs it up with a firm belief in the importance of communication, from the top down and from the bottom up. His door is always open to any and all.

I was reading an article last week about a national bookstore chain that is up for sale. An analyst for one of the New York brokerage houses commented that he had never seen a retail organization as concerned about the bottom line as this book chain. Carl Kroch's philosophy is that the bottom line is not the most important thing in his business life. However, since no business can survive without being profitable, the bottom line is right up there with Jeanette, bookselling, and part ownership of the Cincinnati Reds as things to pay close attention to. I think he has always felt—and the results bear him out—that if you offer a quality selection, quality service, and customer satisfaction, the bottom line would take care of itself.

Years ago, when I was an assistant manager at one of our branch stores, I attended my first K&B Christmas party. These affairs were held in early November, at which time Mr. Kroch would give his annual report and acknowledge the dedication and hard work of all of our managers, assistant managers, and longtime employees. I remember two things from my first party. First, the camaraderie, the feeling of warmth and joy that was everywhere. The open bar may have contributed to these feelings.

The second thing I remember is that I never before had heard anyone, much less the head of a large corporation, stand up in public and acknowledge his love and affection for his wife. You have to remember that this was over twenty years ago, long before we had our sensitivities heightened by all those California witch doctors. I was warmed by the thought that relationships existed that could elicit this kind of public expression. It showed me what we who have worked with him these many years know so well today: that Carl Kroch is a sensitive and caring person.

Nowhere is this more evident than in his philosophy that a great bookstore should be owned and operated by the people who helped make it great, by those who share his philosophy and believe in the traditions he has established. Technically, Mr. Kroch has sold the store to the employees, but I don't remember writing a personal check, so I prefer to think of the "sale" as a gift from a man who is deeply concerned about the future welfare of his employees and about the future of quality bookselling in this country. Since we are "partners" now,

I feel more comfortable expressing my gratitude and appreciation for all that he has done for me directly and by example. I am a bookseller today because of Carl Kroch. Because I am a bookseller, my life has been enriched more than I ever thought possible. I am honored to be part of this tribute to a man who has contributed so much to the community of the book and the community of man.

William McCarthy
chief executive officer,
Kroch's & Brentano's

My point of departure today is this paperback that I hold in my hand: *Fifth Business* by Canadian writer Robertson Davies. It was published in 1970. I located it in one of our branch stores and must say that I was pleased to see that a book published in 1970 was still available in one of our suburban stores. Davies, who is also a playwright, defines "the fifth business" in the beginning of the book. He says, "those roles which be neither those of hero nor heroine, confidante, or villain, which were nonetheless essential to bring about the recognition of the denouement were called fifth business in the drama in the opera companies organized according to the old style. The player who acted these parts was often referred to as fifth business." This prompts two recollections of Carl.

The first one concerns my own opportunity to serve as fifth business. In 1979 I was invited to a breakfast with Roysce Smith, then executive director of the American Booksellers Association, and three publishers: Leona Nevler, Sam Vaughan, and Werner Mark Linz. They told me about The Center for the Book in the Library of Congress and a meeting it was going to hold about publishers and booksellers. They asked me if I could persuade Carl to present a paper

about bookselling. I assured everyone I could. John Cole then followed up with a letter and examples of other papers. But then Carl called me into his office and said, "Bill, what have you gotten me into here?" However, we sat down and talked about it, and especially about the contribution that he felt Kroch's & Brentano's had made over the years. Well, his paper was presented and published, and it was an occasion of great pride for Carl. It also was a moment of pride for me; it was a chance to be a ham for a few minutes—to be the fifth business. But of course we know who the real hero of the drama is.

My second story connected with this book concerns Carl Kroch the bookseller. When *The Fifth Business* was published in 1970, Robertson Davies was not at all known in this part of North America. Kroch's & Brentano's was asked if there was something special it might do. Carl, drawing on the experience of his father, decided to run a full page advertisement in the *Chicago Tribune*, in which the store offered a double your money back guarantee on this book if you didn't feel it was one of the finest introductions to a writer that you had ever read. I do not think that a single book came back. I also feel that the advertisement was one of the reasons why Robertson Davies is now so well known and liked and why his subsequent books have all done so well in

Chicago. This is bookselling as practiced by Carl Kroch and Adolph Kroch. I am very proud to have been associated with it.

Editor's Note

Carl Kroch suffered two personal losses in 1988: his beloved wife Jeanette, who died in February, and William J. McCarthy, Kroch's & Brentano's president and chief executive officer, who died on September 20. McCarthy began his 36-year career at Kroch's & Brentano's in 1952. "Bill represented the best—what Kroch's & Brentano's wants to be. His contribution to the firm was monumental. He was a friend," stated Carl Kroch in a tribute to Bill McCarthy. Kroch named William Rickman, vice-president for merchandise, as the new president and chief operating officer. Rickman, a 25-year Kroch's & Brentano's veteran, had been McCarthy's assistant since 1969.

As part of the transition, Carl Kroch has returned to the store as chief executive officer for a limited period until Rickman assumes the title. Carl Kroch's return has helped fill the void left in his life after his wife's death: "It's wonderful to know I have a place to go," he said. Rickman, a Chicago native, agrees that the return to full-time duties has been a tonic for Carl Kroch: "he needs us and we need him."

Authors

James A. Michener
best-selling author

During my long career I've met with many booksellers—the lifeline of my profession—but none have exceeded Carl Kroch in the warmth with which he met traveling writers in his vast store or in the brazen persistence with which he dogged them for special considerations like autographing huge numbers of books, making personal appearances, and helping him in other ways to promote his store and keep it vital. Because we had such high regard for this energetic man and such respect for his ability to keep a master store alive in difficult times, we acceded to his requests more often than we should have. But we were repaid whenever we reached Chicago and saw that fine establishment still vital, still selling our books, still serving as an important factor in the life of the city.

Harry Mark Petrakis
Chicago author

My first meeting with Carl Kroch came at the time my first novel was published. He had actually read my book and was generous in his praise. The printing was a modest one and the advertising budget Spartan, but Carl did all he could to help it, endorsing it to his book people, recommending it with enthusiasm in his column, "Tending Store".

Through the years I noticed that Carl Kroch was often vigorous and generous in his praise of other books and authors that weren't on any best-seller list but his own. That was a remarkable quality he never lost regardless of the number of bookstores he operated. That was also a quality he cultivated in the good people who worked with him.

On a number of occasions when little-known writers whose books I admired came to Chicago and we visited Kroch's & Brentano's; if Carl were on the premises, he'd always spend a little time with us. My writer friends were treated as his friends. I remember one of them, a poet whose slim book of verse gave him little leverage in the arena of literary commerce, warmed by Carl's friendliness and courtesy, saying about him after we'd left the store, "It was worth coming to Chicago to meet a bookseller like that man."

Lloyd Wendt
Chicago editor and author

Carl Kroch splendidly carries forward
the high traditions of bookselling
launched in Chicago in the early 1830s
by William Bross, the distinguished
bookseller, editor, civic leader, and
later lieutenant governor of Illinois,
who saw accurately that the little wil-
derness town would love books and
grow into greatness. Carl's love of
books, his astute judgment, his excellent Kroch's & Brentano's bookstore,
extended under his guidance into a
vast network, plus his published com-
mentaries and conversations on books,
have made the Chicago metropolitan
area the finest place in the world for
new books to flourish. I've respected
and enjoyed his work as an editor involved in magazines about books, as a
would-be writer, and as president of
the Society of Midland Authors, an organization much concerned with the
fate of young writers as well as established pros. We know Carl as a fair
critic ready to speak out for an obscure
book that has merit in his opinion.
Carl Kroch is the leader among booksellers who have made Chicago a great
book town.

Customers

Ruth F. Boorstin
editor and writer and wife of Daniel J. Boorstin, Librarian of Congress (1975–1987)

Dan and I lived in Chicago for many years and, of course, we were steady customers at Kroch's & Brentano's. As a young faculty wife I often would snoop around to see whether they had a title such as *The Genius of American Politics*, for example. But what I really remember so vividly after all these years are certain clerks in the store. There was a little short woman who seemed to have read every book. Once we were going down to Yucatan and she gave me excellent advice with *such* enthusiasm. That's my strongest memory of Kroch's: you could count on the clerks to find you the right book.

Herman Kogan
historian

Long before the Fast-Buck and Doodad Vendors moved into the field, Carl Kroch was hewing to the traditions established by his father, Adolph, nearly a century ago in Chicago.

He has seen to it that the people he employed—and still does—knew their business, knew books and authors, and were prepared, and well-prepared, to serve customers' needs with efficiency and even ardor. In doing so, they were—and still are—showing a respect for people who write books and a willingness to aid them in snaring the attention of potential readers of their works. This has been true not only for the producers of Best Sellers but for First-Timers whose work has had special interest for Carl and/or his top people. That is a rarity in the book business, as Carl himself remains a kind of rarity.

There are many differences between Carl and the Fast-Buck Boys but, above all, there is a sense of joy and pleasure for an author—and therefore for customers—to bask in the aura of joviality and enthusiasm that is a reflection of the spirit of Carl himself.

Publishers and Booksellers

George P. Brockway
former chairman of W.W. Norton &
Company

Carl Kroch deserves all honor, not only for his role in the development of a great bookstore, but also for making it possible for the employees of that store, who also played roles in its development, to buy it and nourish it after his retirement. I have seen employee ownership work at W.W. Norton & Company; and in my new incarnation as an economist, I am convinced that some such organization of business is best both for the individual company and for the society as a whole.

While Kroch's & Brentano's may not have pioneered in-store book signings, it has become nationally known for them—as a recent Spiderman comic attests. © 1988 *Marvel Entertainment Group, Inc. All rights reserved.*

Herbert B. Fried
former president, Chas. Levy Co.

Carl is the quintessential bookseller. His love and respect for books and his belief that the selling of books is a public service come through loud and clear the moment one steps into a Kroch's & Brentano's store. Like his father before him, Carl saw his mission to be making the widest variety of knowledge, in the form of the printed word, available to the widest number of people. In this day and age he is one of that very small group of booksellers who see themselves as members of an honorable profession, not just purveyors of another grocery product.

I have known Carl since that day in 1952 when he, backed-up by his trusted general manager, Wendell Goodpasture, decided to throw caution to the winds—thereby shocking the publishing world—and stock a full line of low-priced mass-market paperback books. It was a full line, because in typical Carl Kroch fashion he intended to and did give his customers thousands of titles, with something for everybody.

In his own way, Carl is a stubborn man—stubborn in the sense that he had no intention to go along with the crowd. No matter what anybody else was going to do about discounting or selling only the most popular of books, he was not going to be dissuaded from making the widest assortment of reading available to the public at large.

Carl has never wanted to be the biggest, he has just wanted to be the best, and in that no one can doubt his success. Publishers look to him as a fount of information and seek his advice; fellow booksellers look at his success as an inspiration, (possibly tinged with a bit of envy); and his customers find each Kroch's & Brentano's store a wonderfully warm, friendly and welcome place to browse and shop.

As long as Carl is around, it will always be this way.

Laurence Kirshbaum
Warner Books

As a young man I grew up in Chicago
and spent a great deal of time on the
lower merchandise floor (or "basement," as I used to call it, to Carl's cha-
grin) of Kroch's & Brentano's. Of
course this is the location of the paperback section. I spent much of my early
fortune, money that I probably should
have been spending on baseball cards
or Snickers' bars, on books. When I finally got into the book business, it
seemed natural that I gravitated to the
paperback side. The people at Random House, seeing that I was *very*
green, suggested I go out into the field
and try to learn a few things. And
sure enough, they dispatched me to
Chicago, my hometown, and to
Kroch's & Brentano's for a couple of
weeks of training. Ray Carroll taught
me the Kroch's inventory system,
taught me how to count stock, and in
general whipped me into shape. In
those few weeks, I learned, to coin a
corny commercial, how to sell books
"the old-fashioned way:" as personal,
one-on-one gifts of knowledge that
people give to each other or buy for
themselves. We owe much of what the
book business is today to Carl Kroch
and to his family at Kroch's &
Brentano's. My hat is off to you, Carl.

Dana Pratt
director of publishing,
Library of Congress

I take pride in having started out in the
book business as a book peddler: a
salesman from a publisher to a bookseller. My first jobs were in the
midwest, and one of the first persons I
called on was W.W. Goodpasture at
Kroch's & Brentano's, who was known
throughout the book world as
"Goody." In those days I was too
much of a rookie to ever have met Carl
Kroch, but I met Goody because his
business was to buy books from book
salesmen, rookie or veteran. He had to
entertain daily visits, of varying
veracity and specificity, in order to
decide what to buy for the store. He
did it with great skill and courtesy.
But what I remember best was a sign
on Goody's desk that faced all
salesmen and, I now see, reflected the
self-confidence of Kroch's & Brentano's: "I don't give a damn how
many copies Marshall Fields' bought!"

David Replogle
Houghton Mifflin Company

My real respect for Carl comes from
the shape of the institution that he has
built and the people that he selected to
build it. The Wendell Goodpastures,
the Bill McCarthys, the Doris Laufers,
and the others who are carrying on
this great tradition of knowledgeable,
concerned bookselling; not just having
the right books and knowing who
wrote them and what is in them, but
also wanting to guide readers to them.
It is Carl's care for the succession of
the store, his care for his heirs, that I
especially want to honor.

Gail See
proprietor of The Bookcase,
Wayzata, Minnesota,
and former president,
American Booksellers Association

Carl Kroch has always been an
enormous inspiration to booksellers.
In times of great economic and social
change, he has always stood his
ground and given the rest of us the
vision and the will to stand ours. He is
a stubborn man! He has been my hero
and my model for many years. And
he also has influenced my children.
For many years, when my children
were little, we made an annual trip
from Minneapolis to the big city of
Chicago. We would go to the muse-
ums but the final and best visit was
saved for that wonderful store, Kroch's
& Brentano's, on Wabash Avenue.
Each child was allowed to buy one
book, and this is the part of our trip to
Chicago that they remember.

G. Roysce Smith
former executive director,
American Booksellers Association

Carl Kroch is often cited by foreign
booksellers as their model in America.
And no wonder, for Carl is certainly
the most successful independent
bookseller in the history of America.
Moreover, he is fiercely and consistently independent. He is not owned
in part by anybody and never will be.
During Carl's service on the Board of
Directors of the American Booksellers
Association, there were two projects to
which he lent his whole-hearted
support and, in the end, they turned
out to be two of the ABA's best and
most successful projects. They are still
with us today: the ABA Booksellers
School and the ABA monthly magazine, *American Bookseller*.

Section II

Carl Kroch, Bookseller

Carl Kroch promoting new services in 1953.
Kroch's & Brentano's was an innovator in
customer services.

A 'Marco Polo' and His Bookstore

Kevin Kiddoo

Reprinted with permission from AB Bookman's Weekly, *September 23, 1985.*

For Ben Hecht, a young journalist in Chicago, "reading was part of the day. I read constantly. I read on my way to cover stories, while waiting for cardinals to die, murderers to hang, embezzlers to confess, fires to ebb, celebrities to speak. And I bought books as a drunkard orders drinks. I found pleasure not only in reading them but in watching them grow and fill bookshelves and crowd chairs out of corners and lamps off tables."

In that most marvelous autobiography, *A Child of the Century,* Hecht recalls the bookstores whose supplies he devoured: McClurg's, Walter Hill's, the Powner secondhand stores. And then there was "the Marco Polo of Monroe Street in his first hole-in-the-wall bookshop." On his counters "lay all the latest loot of elegance and art. Smiling, young, and gleaming-eyed, this merchant of Monroe Street did not sell me books. Rather he waved a wand and the wonders of de Gourmont, Huysmans, Pollard, Mallarme, Wedekind, D'Annunzio, Villiers de L'Isle-Adam, Strindberg, and Proust sprang into being."

The "Marco Polo of Monroe Street" was affectionately known as Papa Kroch—Adolph Kroch, properly, founder of what is today the premier bookstore in the Windy City and among the foremost in the nation. And it remains a family business: Carl Adolph Kroch, the boss's son, took over in 1952 when his father retired. This year (1985), during which he celebrates fifty years with the company, he and his wife are still the sole owners of Kroch's & Brentano's.

"I have offers probably once a week from people wanting to buy the store," Kroch explains. "I have a very simple form letter which goes: `Kroch's & Brentano's is not for sale.'"

Pretty Ambitious

It was in 1907 that Adolph Kroch, a young immigrant from Austria, founded his German-language bookstore in Chicago. Business went well for him, even into the early years of World War I when he capitalized on the rising unpopularity of all things German among the American public: when Brentano's bookshop decided to sell its $100,000 worth of German-language books, Kroch purchased the entire stock for only $1,000.

But in 1917, with the supply of

German-language books cut off by the blockades, Kroch decided to switch his bookstore's allegiance, too. He telephoned A.C. McClurg, the leading wholesaler and library supplier of the day, and told a salesman he wanted $500 worth of English-language books. "You make the selection," he ordered.

"He was pretty ambitious" recalls his son, who was born in 1914 in what was then German Hospital, but which had by the war's end been renamed Grant Hospital. The elder Kroch moved from store to store—Monroe Street, LaSalle Street, a few locations on Michigan Avenue. Then in 1933 Brentano's went bankrupt. Kroch and a New York investment banker bought the company from a referee in bankruptcy. Although Brentano's had stores around the country—Chicago, New York, Philadelphia, Pittsburgh, Boston, Washington, D.C., among others -- and a book value of more than $1 million, money was scarce in 1933, a Depression year. Kroch and his partner bought out their rival for only $71,000.

Kroch was only interested in the company's Chicago store and in acquiring the right to use the Brentano's name throughout the Midwest. (The unrelated New York store, whose name had since been purchased by Walden Books, recently went bankrupt.) Until 1952, Kroch's and Brentano's were the names of two separate stores in Chicago; only then were they combined into a single entity, and all their operations concentrated in the building that still

Lobby view showing books arrayed in the windows at Kroch's & Brentano's, One North LaSalle Street.

serves as its headquarters at 29 South Wabash Avenue.

The "Meeting Place"

After that move, K&B began an expansion that saw their number of stores grow by almost sixfold. But throughout the thirties and forties their efforts were concentrated on the three Chicago holdings: the two Kroch's stores at Michigan Avenue and LaSalle Street and the Brentano's store that they had acquired in 1933.

Adolph Kroch had graduated from his small first store on Monroe, where he had delighted Ben Hecht and others. He grandly designated his Michigan Avenue store "the Meeting Place of Intellectual Chicago." He left a memorable proof that this was no understatement. In 1927 he started keeping a guest book, in which luminaries ranging across the political and literary spectrum were invited to sign their names and register their comments. "Blessings on the new store" reads the first entry, signed by Will Durant. Flipping the pages, the eye catches the household names: Lowell Thomas, Ernest Hemingway, Carl Sandburg, Thornton Wilder, Noel Coward, Ethel Barrymore.

"Booksellers Are the Chosen of God," prints James Jones. Lady Bird Johnson signed hers, so she said, on "an exciting day." Liberace doodled a piano and candelabra.

Many of the signatures have stories behind them. One day, when President Harry Truman was taking an early morning stroll through Chicago, he peeked into the store's window before opening hours. A porter let him in, and a salesman who recognized the president showed him around. Afterward he dutifully inscribed the guest book. "Thanks for the good `show,'" he wrote, and signed it, "Harry S. Truman, Independence, Mo."

Semi-Rare Books

If anyone knew a thing or two about the brilliance involved in selling a book, it was Adolph Kroch. The Michigan Avenue store generated a sales volume of about $300,000 each year. "When you consider that novels sold then for $2 or at the most $2.50," Carl Kroch considers, "that volume would translate into about $1.5 million today."

It offered a very well-rounded selection. There was a trade department, of course, and children's books, art books, books in foreign languages, and a K&B trademark, the departments centering on technical, scientific and business books.

There were also old and rare books. Kroch describes his father as having been in the "semi-rare book business." He made regular trips to England and the Continent and would stock up on antiquarian items. Neither he nor his son have been book collectors; all his purchases were for the store.

But that type of service isn't practical in his store today, Kroch asserts. It requires a good salesperson, he says, and once you hire one and they acquire a proficiency at the job, they leave to go into business for themselves. A few years ago, K&B sold off all their old books at Swann's in New York, including some "very good" bibliographies of books.

"Things have changed," Kroch observes. "I'd rather sell five hundred $2.50 paperbacks than one $1,000 book. It's nothing for a general bookstore."

Always Planned To Join

Carl Kroch joined his dad's company officially on April 9, 1935, and has stayed with it ever since except for three-and-a-half years in the Navy during World War II. When Papa Kroch retired in 1952 and moved to California, Carl Kroch took over the reins of the company.

Innovations proceeded apace.

K&B had been operating its three traditional stores for two decades, but now entered a period of expansion which has boosted the number of shops to seventeen today. The store in Old Orchard, near Skokie, was "probably the first shopping center bookstore in the country," Kroch estimates. It happened "almost by default"—the developers of the center could not find tenants for one of the stores, so in desperation they offered it to K&B. "I assure you I had a few sleepless nights about it, but it worked out very, very well." There are now fourteen shopping center stores scattered around the greater Chicago area.

When Kroch assumed the helm of K&B, the Brentano's store was managed by W. W. Goodpasture, or "Goody," as he was known. He was responsible for a number of innovative contributions to bookselling. He "persuaded publishers to sell backlist titles on a dating basis so that we could buy and receive those titles in summer and pay for them in January. At first publishers were skeptical, but he asked them, `Would you rather see the books in your warehouse or on our shelves where customers can see them?" His logic won them over, and what we found, of course, was that the books were often sold during the so-called `slow-season,' and we would have to reorder for the holiday season," Kroch recalls.

Full Service

The care taken in selecting new locations for a K&B store, the consid-eration for the customer that led to improved lighting throughout the bookstores—these get to the heart of the philosophy about bookselling at K&B stores.

They call themselves "full-service bookstores," and Kroch has had the expression patented in the U.S. Patent Office, to be used exclusively by Kroch's & Brentano's. "I stole the idea from full-service banks about ten or fifteen years ago, he says with a chuckle. "The best ideas you appropriate from other people."

Each One is Different

This personalized regard for bookselling extends to every store. "We're not a chain," Kroch explains. "We're really a collection of personal bookstores. We give the managers quite a bit of autonomy: every store is different because of the likes and dislikes of the manager. Everyone has his own special interest."

Thus, the South Wabash Avenue store—which does "the largest volume of any single bookstore in the United States"—also has "the leading business, technical and scientific book department of any general bookstore in the country." The Oakbrook store—located in a community where a number of businesses have developed-was fortunate to have as a manager someone interested in computers; it has large computer and finance sections, well-suited to its population. The Oak Park store is in a college community with a lot of young people, and has a manager interested in children's books: its stock includes a generous selection of these.

However strong these stores may get in a particular area, though, they will never evolve into a "specialized" store. Specialization runs against the grain of Carl Kroch's philosophy. So does discounting. The large nation-wide chains stock a comparatively small number of titles—about 5,000 compared with the 125,000 in K&B's South Wabash store—and rely on a large turnover. Kroch's philosophy is, if he can sell three copies of a book during a year, he will stock the book. By stocking more books and training his sales force thoroughly on what items they have available, Kroch feels he can provide a superior service that customers will continue to use long after the competition has gone out of business.

"I don't worry too much about my competition," he says, relaxed. "I figure, you do your own job and let the competition take care of itself." And by not discounting books, he can ensure his customers that K&B will not undersell itself and won't have to compromise its "full service" boast in future years. Remainders now constitute only about 4 percent of K&B's business.

Would he ever consider discount-ing? "I won't say `never'—never is a long time, as Mr. Harry S. Truman said—but I will say I'll be the last one to do it."

What he will do is go to great trouble to provide personalized service for a customer. If a customer wants a book that is out of print, Kroch's and Brentano's will search for it: during one recent year they obtained some 40,000 out-of-print titles for customers. Phil Anderson, who is the buyer of children's books, promotional books, and newspapers and magazines, also handles the out-of-print market for Kroch's and Brentano's, notifying customers that the service is available and using *AB Bookman's Weekly* to search for titles.

K&B even helps other bookstores around the country with their Bookseller's Catalogue Service, a separate entity but one under the K&B umbrella. Out of a pool of 250 to 300 books, about 128 are chosen for inclusion in a catalog that is sold to bookstores that cannot afford to publish their own; they have their names stamped on the covers of their copies for local distribution. Judy Krug, who handles public relations and writes and edits the in-house newsletter *This Week at K&B*, also handles these nationally distributed *Book Chat* catalogs, which go out bimonthly, with a special edition at Christmas. In addition to being sold to other stores around the country, about 90,000 copies are mailed to K&B customers, and another 30,000 are given away at the seventeen stores.

Again: "Gleaming-eyed"

In April 1980 Carl Kroch was invited to read a paper on "The Co-Responsibilities of American Booksell-ers and Publishers" at The Center for the Book in The Library of Congress.

It included some interesting information about his family and the store, as
well as four "controversial" suggestions for future cooperative activities—
for booksellers to receive their books
once again on a nonreturnable basis;
and for publishers, sellers, printers,
and authors to fund a national
advertising campaign to encourage
Americans to read. But he ended his
talk with a quotation from Jeremy
Collier, written in 1698, that suggested
that Carl Kroch was just as "gleaming-
eyed" as his father when it comes to
books, waving his wand every day
over an exciting and innovative
company that has become a landmark
in the Windy City.

Baron of Books

Paul Weingarten

Reprinted with permission from Sunday, The Chicago Tribune Magazine, *December 28, 1986.*

It is a bittersweet time in the life of Carl Kroch, Chicago's legendary bookseller. It is a time of change, a time of stepping down. It is a moment that Kroch has anticipated for several years, being seventy-two now, and a moment that he has avoided for a long as possible. The torch is passing, as it did from Adolph Kroch to his son Carl in 1952. Now it is passing to the employees of the bookstore chain themselves. Carl promises that his bookstore, Kroch's & Brentano's, will not change. In a few years, however, it will no longer be his to promise.

Everyone knows about Kroch's, but fewer know that there is a Carl Kroch. In earlier days he dwelled in the shadow of his well-known father. But it was Carl who propelled a small family firm into what once was the largest bookstore chain in America. The chain was small by today's standards—a dozen stores or so—but it had clout in the days when the vast majority of bookstores in America were minor-league operations. Publishers, authors, and salesmen paid their respects to Carl Kroch. He was,

as one publisher put it, "Mr. God."

It could not remain that way because Carl Kroch was unwilling to think like others in the book business. He was unwilling to cut corners on service, unwilling to do business any way other than the way it had been done since his father founded the store in 1907.

In those days the book business was considered a gentleman's calling, a tidy and honorable way to make a living. In the last decade, however, the book business has been nothing short of war. And in that time Kroch's has found itself caught in a pincer movement--first the proliferation of the national chains B. Dalton Bookseller and Walden Book Company Inc., and then the slashing attack of discounter Crown Books Corp. Together these forces dethroned Carl Kroch.

Dethroned, yes. Destroyed, no. Today the war continues, and Kroch's continues. It even thrives as the fifth largest chain in the country. Sales remain steady, and Kroch remains committed to his way of doing things. That means you will always find clerks who know something about books in Kroch's, you will always find books beyond—way beyond—this week's best-sellers, and you will always find a certain sense of tradition. What you will not find is the latest marketing techniques, the high-tech ordering and delivery systems, or the deep discounts that others offer.

He may not be No. 1, but Carl Kroch still does things his way, the old fashioned way.

That goes for his personal life, too.

Carl Kroch's limousine is a deep burgundy, almost black. The door carries his initials, CAK, in flowery script. Carl Adolph Kroch glides along in back, Buddha-like, resplendent in a handmade Italian suit and fedora.

Just before noon the limo carries Kroch from his office at Kroch's & Brentano's on Wabash Avenue to lunch, usually the Tavern Club, and 333 North Michigan Avenue. His father was one of the first members of the club, founded in 1928; Carl joined in 1947.

Every afternoon the limo ferries him to his Lake Shore Drive apartment, in the same building that he and his wife Jeanette—he calls her Jet— have occupied since 1939. He likes to get home in time to watch the television game show "Jeopardy."

Carl Kroch talks. A single question triggers a half-hour spiel on the highlights of fifty-one years in the book business ("I remember the first paperback, *Lost Horizon*, which sold for 25 cents, and the first $3 novel, *Gone with the Wind*. We all said it wouldn't sell"), his opinions on the management of the Cincinnati Reds, of which he owns a one-fifteenth share, and brief history of his exploits as a World War II naval officer, all mixed with various bits of trivia gleaned form a lifetime of scanning four or five books a week.

But beyond the standard bio, Carl Kroch is not easy to crack. "He's a very private person," his friends will tell you. "He cultivates a serene, statesmanlike image. Is Kroch, in Kroch's estimation, a tough businessman? "I don't think I am," he says softly. Can you stay in business without being tough? "You sure as hell can," he says, voice rising a notch.

Carl Kroch can be extremely charming or he can flashfreeze you with a single glance. He radiates kinetic energy; he seems to be in a hurry even when sitting still. The first day he arrived at Cornell, in 1935, freshman Kroch strode into the Beta Theta Pi fraternity house in such a manner, his sister says, as to earn a nickname that would follow him throughout his life: The Baron.

It has been suggested in the past that Carl Kroch's lifestyle is a bit too grand. Specifically, it has been suggested on three separate occasions since 1971, the first time K & B employees—many of whom make little more than minimum wage—were solicited to join a union.

Each time, the proposal was soundly defeated. But Kroch took it hard. "He took it as a personal affront," says a former employee. "I don't think he ever got over it."

Kroch knows he is vulnerable. He says: "They (the union organizers) would say, 'Well, look, Carl Kroch rides around in a limousine, and you have to scrimp and this and that.'"

Well, he does live in a style reminiscent of "The robber barons?" he says. A smile fades quickly. "I feel I've earned it. And I was fortunate that I inherited a pretty good hunk of money. My father probably made more in the retail book business than anyone before or since. I feel I deserve it."

"Carl Kroch has everything," says a longtime friend, Dr. Harold Method, Tribune Company medical director. He neglects to mention that most of it seems to be crammed into Kroch's library at home, much to the horror of his wife. There, Kroch has Matisse etchings, a copy of *Ulysses* autographed by James Joyce and a plastic clock in the shape of the United States, a promotional gift for the movie *Rocky IV*. "It stands next to the fifteen-inch statue of Ezra Cornell, which Kroch received in 1982 after he endowed the position of university librarian, for $1 million, at his alma mater. Nearby is his collection of colored golf balls from around the world.

"A lot of this stuff has absolutely no significance," Kroch offers cheerfully. "But I love the room. It's my inspiration."

Kroch still rises at five-thirty, reads the papers and then exercises for twenty minutes, following a routine in a book called "Miss Craig's 21-Day Shape-Up Program." He has done so for at least twenty years.

He's in the office by nine. The office is actually two offices—one for show, one for work. The show office has Japanese art on the walls and neutral-colored decorative Oriental screens on the windows to obscure the "L" tracks. This is where Kroch entertains visiting authors. A large portrait of his wife overlooks his eight-foot oval Brazilian rosewood desk.

Here are the framed proclamations and certificates and appreciations from a lifetime of bookselling. Here also is a bronze bust of Adolph Kroch. And photos: Carl by Karsh (the famous photographer), Carl and Jet, Carl and Jet and Nancy Reagan.

Yousuf Karsh book signing at Kroch's & Brentano's, 1970.

One wall is filled with books, mostly cookbooks. He doesn't cook, "but as you can see, I like the results. I like to read cookbooks. You learn about different cultures. Who said you learn more from eating habits of people than anything else?"

Kroch works in an adjacent cubbyhole. A couch is piled high with books. He has an ancient Smith-Corona typewriter, a digital clock that registers to a tenth of a second, another wall of cookbooks.

Wherever he goes, Carl Kroch is never far from the past. The benign gaze of his late father follows him from room to room; ditto his late mother. They remind him of simpler times, perhaps. In those days, the main competition was the department stores, mostly Marshall Field & Co.

"We laughed when we heard that B. Dalton was talking about having seventy-five stores," Kroch recalls. "That seemed so ridiculous at the time."

The chains' strategy in 1966 was simple: Go into every shopping mall, put stores in small towns that never had a bookstore before. In the beginning, Walden, headquartered in Connecticut, concentrated on the east, and Dalton, in Minneapolis, the west. Eventually, they met in the middle.

The first Chicago-area Walden opened in 1968 in the Yorktown shopping center in Lombard. The first Dalton came three years later at Woodfield mall in Schaumburg.

In the 1970s the two mushroomed. Walden for example, had 250 stores by early 1973, 500 by 1978 and 750 only three years after that. The chain, sold to K Mart Corp. in 1984, expects to open store number 1,000 this year. It has 27 stores in the Chicago area. (Recently, Dayton Hudson put the chain up for sale.)

Within a few years, Kroch's share of the market, once 30 percent in Illinois, declined to its current 20 percent. "Carl hated the chains," says a former employee. "He didn't want anyone coming in and taking anything away." But the chains did more than slice into Kroch's business: They expanded the overall book market far beyond expectations. For example, the sale of hardcover trade books—which includes just about everything but textbooks—surged from $444 million in 1972 to almost $2 billion last year.

One former Dalton store manager in Chicago reveals how the corporation viewed Kroch's as competition: "The general impression I got was (Kroch's was thought to be) kind of old-fashioned fuddy-duddies, not keeping up with the times, and it would be easy to plow over them. There was a lot propaganda to store managers, that once B. Dalton dropped its machinery in place, it could dominate the market."

The B. Dalton at 129 North Wabash Avenue, however, "was not a particularly charming or comfortable environment," the manager recalls. "It had twenty-five-foot ceilings and pipes hanging out. It was definitely a supermarket atmosphere. Our sales were good, but we certainly weren't plowing over them."

The Dalton manager scouted Kroch's regularly. "We paid a lot attention to what they were promoting and when they got their books. That's a hot issue all the time. Who got James Michener first. It's usually a matter of a day or two. If it is more than that, the publisher is going to die.

"Kroch's always had top preference for getting autograph appearances. Again, they had historic ties with the publishers, and they did a great job with them, and a lot of times they'd get authors we didn't get, or they'd get them first.

Meanwhile, Carl Kroch did something his father never envisioned: He expanded form three stores in 1953 to 16 by 1973, to lay claim to a slice of the expanding market.

In 1981 the competition grew even more fierce. Crown Books opened its first Chicago branch, almost across the street from Kroch's. The discounting of best-sellers, which is Crown's stock in trade, is particularly repugnant to Kroch, who, along among the top five bookselling chains, has refused to follow. "I can't afford to," he says. "This is no longer entirely my decision; I can't say I'll never discount, but I'll be the last one, which I practically am. If we would sell books at the prices that Crown does, the only person that would be getting a cent would be our landlord. Why should I do that? I'd rather not have the business."

The book business, as Kroch often points out, operates on paper-thin margins. Unlike clothing, for example, where markups are typically 100 percent, the average markup on books is 40 to 45 percent. Kroch claims his expenses, or overhead, is about 40 percent, which leaves little room for discounting. Indeed, he says Kroch's sales volume has been flat for two years; other sources say it is more like five years. Overall sales figures have similarly been estimated at $34 million

to $44 million, probably closer to the former.

When Crown arrived in Chicago, Kroch's first strategy was to ignore it. When asked about discounting soon after Crown opened, he replied icily, "I have nineteen stores, and I have nineteen no comments."

Today Kroch has seventeen stores, Crown has 198, and he has taken a different tack. He has seen his best-seller business evaporate—by his own estimate down 60 percent. But he maintains that was only a tiny percentage of his business anyway. Kroch changes the slogan of his store from "World's Largest Bookstore" to "The Full Service Bookstores," and trade-marked it in 1974.

Kroch's is a store about which term old-fashioned can be a compliment—or not. "There are different philosophies in the book business," says Kroch's chief executive officer William McCarthy. "We're dealing with one philosophy, and a lot of other people are dealing with another, which is just to sell a product, like you do liver and bacon, across the counter. Their philosophy is to make a buck off this product. We have a philosophy, which is to make a buck, too, but to do it in a different way."

It is different. Kroch's continues to stress service and a 100,000-title selection of books, while the giant national chains like B. Dalton and Walden are cutting back. The store orders at least 30,000 of the 40,000 or so new titles published every year, for example, compared to half that at

Walden's. Kroch's departments of art, science and technical, and business books are unparalleled in the city perhaps the country.

At Kroch's they still sell books the old-fashioned way. "If you go to the chains with a book that they know the publisher has a deep interest in," says one publishing executive, "their response sometimes is something stupid like, 'How much money are you going to throw at it (for advertising)?' Kroch's doesn't work that way. They're smarter. They know that throwing money at books doesn't make books sell. It's publishing books well—that is, making sure the book gets reviewed, getting authors on talk shows, making the cover attractive, making it attractively priced."

McCarthy is one of a highly respected cadre of top Kroch's executives. His mentor was the late W.W. Goodpasture, a legend in bookselling. "Goody" was well known for his bookselling acumen. In 1952, for example, Goody decided that there was a future in paperback books, and Kroch's opened a "Super Book Mart" with a then-astounding 15,000 titles.

Goody was also known for flamboyantly loud sports jackets.

McCarthy, by contrast, wears gray suits. He has a studious, vaguely distracted mien, a dry sense of humor and a voice that rarely strays form a low monotone. McCarthy spent a year as a substitute schoolteacher; the students nicknamed him Mr. Peepers because of the black horn-rimmed eyeglasses that he still favors. He joined Kroch's in 1952. "I thought I was fairly good as a clerk," he says. "I had some background in literature and certain departments were turned over to me, including natural history, and I had to memorize all the books on mushrooms. There were about twenty at the time."

When McCarthy visits the competition, "if I'm very well waited on, I get madder than hell," he jokes. "But then on the other hand, I say, 'That's terrific'" It doesn't happen that often, he says. "I had one case [of superb service] in a Walden store," he recalls. The store has since closed. "They gave too much service, I guess."

On the other hand, old-fashioned can sometimes mean behind the times. "No corporation with a board of directors and stockholders would run a corporation this way," says a former employee, who describes an antiquated, cumbersome system of unpacking and repacking books to supply the branch stores.

The fiscal year that ended June 30, Carl Kroch says, "was the biggest year in our history, this in spite of all the prophets of doom you hear." If Kroch has regrets about not going national, he does not betray them. "I had given it a certain amount of thought. I would have had a big store in the central business district of various big cities, and then satellite stores. Then I finally decided, well, there's just so much money a person needs, you can just have so many martinis, so many sirloin steaks, and this way I can be home every night, I don't have those added worries. Twenty years ago, perhaps I should have done it, but I have everything I want."

It is 11:45, time for lunch. On the way to the club to meet Jeanette, he says: "I have a lot of fun, what the hell. You might as well in life. You say why didn't I own a thousand stores—and have a thousand worries?"

Is he still angry about the discounters? "I'm really not that type of person," he says. "I guess that's why I don't have ulcers. What good does it do to become angry?" And he changes the subject, to his favorite: Jet.

Kroch is not one to get overly sentimental. He is not one to get sentimental at all, except about Jet. Portraits of her in the 1940's through the 1970s dominate the landscape—in his office, his den, his living room, his hallways.

Invariably, in a conversation about the early years, a friend will say Kroch was a bit wild. And then they will say, "Then he met Jeanette." There are clearly two periods in Kroch's life: before Jeanette and after Jeanette. He was smitten and remains smitten. He speaks often of his "happy home life."

Does he bring work home?

"No," says Jet. She is impeccably dressed in silk, her short white hair perfectly coiffed.

"We discuss things a lot," Carl interrupts. "Jet's been tremendously helpful. For example, when the Water Tower project was going on, we didn't sign a lease because I thought it was too expensive, and Jet said, 'You have to have a store there.' And we did, and it's been tremendously successful. Women's intuition often is quite helpful."

Kroch loves to eat, and Jet hates to cook. He jokes that Jet's idea of cooking is buying cold cuts. Given this situation, he and his wife take most meals at the Tavern Club.

At lunch Carl and Jet talk about their first date. Jet was a nightclub dancer, a State Lake Sweetheart, along with her twin sister Jean; Carl was fresh out of Cornell.

"We met March 20, 1936," Kroch says proudly.

"It was a blind date," says Jeanette.

"And I was blind," Kroch says.

What happened?

"Nothing," says Kroch with a laugh. He took her to his sister's birthday, and so I wasn't too happy," Jeanette recalls, implying that Kroch was not on his best behavior. "He wasn't fresh, but I didn't like anyone drinking that much. Then he was so nice the next day, he sent me orchids."

Jeanette and her sister became Chez Paree "Adorables" in 1937, after their request for a $5 raise at the State Lake was denied.

Jet and Carl dated for three years. Their schedules collided, but Carl was always welcome at the Chez. "Mike Fritzel (the owner) knew who the girls were going out with," Jet recalls, "and he didn't care much for musicians or gamblers."

They married on August 12, 1939.

Carl Kroch has seen many things change. Even the American Booksellers Association, a chummy, old boys' network, was scandalized in 1984 by the first successful write-in campaign in its eighty-six-year history. Four "radicals" were elected to the board by a landslide write-in vote. Their radical notion: The ABA should pay more attention to independent booksellers and less to chains.

In 1984 the ABA also started a system called BOS—Booksellers Order System—by which small independents could pool their orders and qualify for the larger discounts that the chains routinely received.

In this battle, Kroch's is now more an independent that a chain. The difference between the real chains and Kroch's is elegantly embodied in one Kroch's sales clerk, Grace Peterson.

"Those (chain) places are like supermarkets," she says. "If you go in there and ask for something, they'll point in some vague direction, and if you can find the book, fine."

That is not the way she does it.

Grace Peterson sells books. She is spry and birdlike, just having celebrated her seventy-ninth birthday. She retired thirteen years ago after thirty-two years at Marshall Field's. "At that time, when you were sixty-five, you were just put up on a shelf, you weren't worth anything anymore," she observes. "I'd be really lost without this (job)."

Peterson has a following of loyal customers, for whom she suggests titles. "They call periodically and say, 'What do you have for me to read, you know what I like,' and that kind of thing." She chats with her customers about their families, hobbies and favorite recipes. One of her regulars lives in New York. "She could go right down the street in New York and get anything, but she calls me," Peterson says.

Perhaps some of it is due to a strict Peterson policy: "If people don't like what I send them, they're free to return it. I don't always hit it right, I mean, I'd rather they tell me. Because I don't want them to have something they don't want." Very few books come back.

Upstairs at Kroch's is Henry Tabor, a thirty-three-year veteran at Kroch's who calls himself "the world's oldest stock boy." He later admits to being manager of the huge art book department.

Tabor conducts his business behind a Formica desk that bears the signatures, in grease pencil, of various artists who have come to visit: Dr. Seuss, illustrator Franklin McMahon, naturalist Roger Tory Peterson.

Tabor is diminutive, almost elfin in his well-tailored suit and Prince Valiant haircut. "We take Visa, MasterCard, American Express, wampum, bargain beads, or I'll toss you for it," he tells a potential customer. He says he doesn't know how many books are in the department. He knows the most expensive is "Modern Japanese Prints," a set by James Michener, for $7,500. Asked about his customers, he exits and returns with a two-foot card file crammed with cards, each containing the name of a customer.

"These are my family, my extended family," he says, plunking the card file on the table. Correction: These are his family, A to H. You can pick cards at random, and Tabor knows each person.

Tabor still remembers lessons he learned from Adolph Kroch. Recently he put a book titled *Tattoo* in the window of the Wabash store. He suspected, rightly, that it would appeal to the punk underground. They sold fifty copies, at $60 per, by word of mouth.

"The window still has great attraction," he says. "When I first started, we had a location at 206 North Michigan. Mr. Adolph Kroch, who would still come by to visit, would check out the window, and if he found exposed areas of carpeting (in the window) he wanted to know if you were selling carpeting or books."

The rapid expansion of the major chains in the 1970s ended with the current glut of shopping malls. "Ten

Kroch's Bookstore, 206 North Michigan Avenue, before 1933.

years ago we could open 100 stores in new malls; this year it's maybe 15 or so," says John Bradbury, vice president for real estate at Dalton. Dalton and Walden have begun discounting best-sellers, which has cut already thin profit margins. It has also hurt Crown, which showed a net gain of only two stores from May 1985 to May 1986. Crown had planned to have 210 stores by the end of the year but will fall eleven short of that target.

The pressures are such that chain booksellers talk more and more about generating what they call fast "turns"—turnover of merchandise. "Books don't sell fast enough," laments Bradbury. "But if we want to be a complete bookstore, we have to have books that don't sell fast enough. Like a hardware store that has to carry all the nuts and bolts but only sells quarter-inch."

That, however, is subject to change, if you can read between the lines. "We're making an effort to streamline our inventory but not to the detriment of the customer," Bradbury says. The store is trimming its typical 25,000 title inventory, "getting rid of those items that are just not being called for." In other words, the books that don't sell fast enough.

In many stores, books have been losing space to higher-profit items such as computer software, audio and video cassettes, magazines, games, puzzles, mugs, stationery, and cards. Walden has even decided to emphasize what it calls "plush"—corporate jargon for stuffed animals.

At Kroch's a quarter of the sales come from nonbook items such as greeting cards, games, mugs, and tapes. Kroch's is now a place where you can find a two-volume set of "Ceramic Industries of Medieval Nubia," for $75, and one floor below, a wide selection of audio cassettes, including a rack of "Subliminal Persuasion—Self Hypnosis" tapes with titles such as "So, You're Out of a Job," "Stop Bed-Wetting," and "Develop Enthusiasm."

Enthusiasm was Adolph Kroch's secret to selling. "Dad could have sold anything," says Carl. "His philosophy was enthusiasm. He said be enthusiastic (because) without enthusiasm your knowledge doesn't do you any good."

Adolph Kroch came to America from Lemberg, Austria (now L'vov, USSR), in 1902. The official story is that he came to escape a life of banking that his father had envisioned for his son. The unofficial story is that he may have come here to evade the draft. On the trip over, the twenty-year-old Austrian lost most of his modest bankroll, swindled by another passenger.

He landed on Christmas Eve and immediately set off for Chicago, there to indulge his passion for books. He tried to find work at a bookstore but failed. "So he went to Milwaukee," Carl recalls, "because he thought it was a German town where he had a greater opportunity of getting a job. And he passed by a factory, and it said, 'Bookkeeper wanted.' All he knew was the 'book' part of it; he knew nothing about accounting. It was the Milwaukee Sash and Door Co., as I remember, and they didn't hire him as a bookkeeper but as a factory employee, and he worked there for a number of months. I'm surprised that he still had all his fingers because he was very uncoordinated."

After several months, he was offered a bookselling job in Chicago, and "as he tells the story, I'm sure it's true, he didn't even wait until the end of the week when he got his paycheck. He rushed right down to Chicago and went to work for Koelling and Klappenbach on Randolph Street."

He rose from clerk to salesman, and after five years, he started his own store at 26 Monroe Street. A. Kroch & Co. was a German-language bookstore until World War I stanched the flow of books. In 1917 Adolph Kroch placed an order for $500 worth of English-language books. They sold so well that he soon abandoned the German-book business. In the next decades he helped invent the modern book business by innovative practices such as convincing publishers to ship extra books "for display" and then allow the return of unsold books for credit.

His bookstore became a literary mecca. In Ben Hecht's autobiography, *Child of the Century*, he recalled Kroch as "Marco Polo of Monroe Street...On Papa Kroch's counters lay all the latest loot of elegance and art. Smiling, young, and gleaming eyed, this merchant of Monroe Street did not sell me books. Rather he waved a wand, and the wonders of deGourmont, Huysmans, Pollard...Strindberg and Proust sprang into being."

The guest register from the opening of his first Michigan Avenue store, 206 North, on December 10, 1927, bears the signatures of Ernest Hemingway, Will Durant, Ben Hecht, Charles MacArthur, Carl Sandburg, and Thornton Wilder.

In 1933 Adolph Kroch and a partner bought the bankrupt New York-based bookstore chain Brentano's at auction for $71,000. The price astounded Kroch; the value of the chain's inventory alone was well over $1 million. After several years the partners split, not amicably, and Adolph Kroch retained the Brentano store in Chicago area. The names were merged by Carl in 1952, the same year the Wabash Store became trademarked as the "World's Largest Bookstore."

Meanwhile, Carl had graduated from Francis W. Parker School in 1931 and enrolled at Cornell University. He cut a rakish figure, with his Packard Roadster and a full-length raccoon coat. He was an engineering major, known to "borrow" certain chemicals

Kroch's & Brentano's developed the Brentano's Book Chat *into the suberb bimonthly catalog issued today.*

50

from the lab in order make what was known as "bathtub gin." "He was just your average hell-raiser," recalls long-time friend Mrs. Elizabeth Heekin, who met Kroch at Cornell.

He intended to be a chemical engineer and had completed two years of courses. "I think when you're a youngster, you kind of resent your family's business and think you're going to set the world on fire in something else," Kroch says. In his junior year his resolve began to waver. "I think one of the things that might have made me reconsider was that on the bulletin board in the chemistry building were all kinds of people looking for jobs, doctors of chemical engineering, at $100 a month."

"Carl adored our father," says his sister, Gretchen. "He really wanted to do anything to please him. My father never pushed him, but he hoped." After graduation in 1935 Kroch started as a clerk at the 206 North Michigan Avenue store. His father taught him the first lesson: how to alphabetize books. (Arrange them in stacks from a to f, g to k, l to r and s to z.)

The same year, he collaborated on his first and only book. It is a slender tome, a parody of a then-best-seller called *So Red the Rose*. Kroch's version was entitled *So Red the Nose, or Breath in the Afternoon*. It revealed the favorite cocktail recipes of thirty authors, including Erskine Caldwell, Edgar Rice Burroughs, Frank Buck, Irving Stone, Theodore Dreiser, Harriet Monroe, and Ernest Heming-way. (Hemingway's cocktail, dubbed

"Death in the Afternoon": "1 jigger of absinthe into a champagne glass. Add iced champagne until it attains the proper opalescent milkiness. Drink 3 to 5 of these slowly.") "That one is drinkable," Kroch says. "Some of them are actually suicidal."

Kroch and four college chums also formed a very exclusive club called TULLA—The Urban Liquor Lovers of America. They would meet on a half-acre private island in the Thousand Island, a chain of minuscule islands on the St. Lawrence Seaway near the mouth of Lake Ontario. "Carl thought up TULLA," recalls William "Joe" Williams, who owned the island. Williams is president of Western and Southern Life Insurance Co., head-quartered in Cincinnati. "We would meet up there for several weeks every summer. Carl had shirts printed up. He was the vice-president. Oh, we had a great time. Our meetings never seemed to break up. We'd get into a red dog game and could play that all night."

At work, Kroch and his father didn't often clash. One difference of opinion, however, involved Dale Carnegie's *How to Win Friends and Influence People*. Adolph Kroch ordered 25,000 copies, "an unheard-of order for us in those days," Carl recalls. "I said, 'Dad, you're going to insult our customers (with that book),' which just shows how wrong I was." Kroch's sold upwards of 75,000 copies, and it still sells.

World War II interrupted the younger Kroch's career. He was

commissioned an ensign in the Navy and found himself on the U.S.S. Osterhaus, a naval destroyer escort in the South Pacific. He was an engineering officer, a position complicated by the fact that "I had never seen a diesel engine in my life."

In 1952, at the age of seventy, Adolph Kroch retired to Laguna Beach, California. Carl was thirty-eight years old. He remained close to his father, phoning him daily. He relied on the counsel of the aforementioned W.W. Goodpasture, and together the two sold a lot of books. They created a new kind of bookstore, one with more lighting to brighten up the traditionally dark bookstore atmosphere. They also realized that the typical bookrack concealed a book's most valuable selling asset, its cover. So Kroch developed racks with shelves tilted to display full book covers.

In 1957 Kroch's began expanding. Old Orchard. Oak Park. Oakbrook mall. River Oaks. Evergreen Plaza. By 1966 he had expanded to 10 stores, the largest bookstore chain in America.

Adolph Kroch died in 1978 at the age of ninety-six. His son had the obituary bronzed. It hangs on a wall in his office.

Kroch's & Brentano's could launch a best-seller. Kroch's is credited with propelling William Martin's 1981 novel, *Back Bay* to best-seller status. "Any publisher will tell you that for a long time we have always turned to Kroch's when we needed help to get a book going," says Carl Apollonio, vice

president of sales for Crown Publishing Group. "In our case it was *Back Bay*. Mr. Kroch read that book, and he got very excited about that, and they decided really to get behind it. Mr. Kroch ran a major ad, saying to his customers he was recommending the book, and if they were disappointed, he would give them double their money back."

Today, if Kroch's alone cannot make a best-seller, it can at least get things rolling. An example is *Henry Miller: Full of Life*. Even though Kroch is not a fan of Miller, he started reading the book and found it "fascinating. Miller was really a despicable character. I mean he went to the depths, almost lived in the sewers of Paris. He would take advantage of his friends, always trying to cadge money. So here's a kind of book you like to get your hands on. A book that the chains probably won't even carry. There won't be any advertising for it. I'm sure it will be well-reviewed, and we might be able to get that book going. It's never going to be a best-seller, but that doesn't matter. If we can sell a couple thousand copies in Chicago, I think we've done something."

Kroch is evasive about naming his favorite writers, tending to mention the one he reading at the moment. At this moment, it is Pat Conroy, author of *The Great Santini* and a new novel, *Prince of Tides*. "I think he's going to be one of the real comers. He's a little pretentious, that's my only criticism. But he writes a hell of a story."

Kroch does admit that he is not a

big fan of the trasherati such as Sidney Sheldon or Judith Krantz. He will boast of encouraging Chicago writer Harry Mark Petrakis after his first novel flopped. And he speaks fondly of Margaret Truman—"a charming person. Her photos don't do her justice."

Kroch's reading list is a catholic affair, although it tends to nonfiction. Recently he was in the middle of *Shootdown*, about the Soviet downing of the Korean Air airliner, *The Invisible Billionaire*, a biography of billionaire Daniel Ludwig; and *Ford: The Men and the Machine*, about the automobile-family dynasty. As for mysteries, Kroch has a friend who screens all of those and recommends a few.

Kroch remains alert to the latest fads. "Right now," he announces, "the hottest thing in the book business is loons. Any book you publish on loons sells. And we must have a dozen now." Books on running, macrame, nouvelle cuisine, and houseplants seem to be ebbing, while quilting is coming on.

Such are the vagaries of the business. "There was a best-seller in 1935 called *The Seven Pillars of Wisdom*, written by T.E. Lawrence," Kroch recalls. "And it was $5, and I tried to read the book and found it impossible to do so. And I went to my father and I said, 'Dad, why are people buying this book?' He said, 'All of a sudden everyone wants to have a copy on their coffee table.'"

Carl Kroch receives dozens of books a week from hopeful publishers. On his desk now is *The Soviet Paradox* from Random House. It came with a personal letter from the publisher, Robert Bernstein. "Bernstein thinks it's the best book on Soviet-American relations that he's read. He'd like me to read it." If Kroch reads it and likes it, then he will get behind it, perhaps by displaying it in the window or ballyhooing it in the store's free in-house pamphlet *Book Chat*.

If the book really catches on, other independents, and possibly even the chains, may order it. The chains order huge quantities of books and distribute them nationwide with the help of computers. At Kroch's, computers, for certain limited tasks, came only five years ago. Inventory is still done by hand.

Julia Pheiffer, director of sales and marketing for Chicago-based Contemporary Books Inc., says: "We do regional books for (Walden), specialized books. And they have their stores sorted in all kinds of ways. We had a fish cookbook this summer, and the buyer said, 'Let me see the table of contents.' And he took a look at it, and he said, 'We'll send this to both our freshwater and saltwater stores.'"

All this technology, of course, is not invincible. Recently, B. Dalton revealed that several million dollars' worth of books were present on the computer inventory but AWOL from the shelves. In other words, the books weren't on the shelves, but the computer didn't know it. As a result, Dalton has a new system of buying and distributing books, and several new faces in top management.

Walden reportedly has also had problems with computers, all of which makes Kroch feel extremely cautious about new technology. "We were hooked up for three or four years to a computer base of all books in print (some 600,000 titles). So if you'd come in and said, 'What is available by Hemingway?' we'd put it in the computer, and out would come 200 titles. This was great, but what the hell use was it? What good would it be for use to know that *The Sun Also Rises* is available in three editions? You gotta be practical."

While Kroch's snails its way into the computer era, the chains streak ahead. The result can be a severe case of whiplash. Walden, for instance, has gone from centralized buying of books to decentralized buying, back to cen-tralized, and is now again decentraliz-ing. Walden's director of merchandise buying, Anne Simon, says: "This fall, for the first time, stores are determin-ing their own stock level on backlist everything but new best-sellers). On frontlist, new books, we're still doing the buying. But we're opening it up more and more because we realize that each (store has a different) customer base. The stores are ecstatic; they're no longer standing in back rooms opening boxes, saying, 'Those people must be on drugs.'"

Walden is also promoting book clubs—children's, science fiction, mystery—a concept that Kroch's tried and abandoned twenty-five years ago. "If you listen to some of these guys in New York, they're out there trying to rediscover the wheel or something," says William McCarthy. "And you'd think that anybody who's been here for the last fifty years is a bunch of idiots and morons."

The battle lines, Kroch says, are clearly drawn: full service versus bottom line. Who will win? "I think both sides are going to win," he says.

But won't the chains try to destroy Kroch's? "They don't believe in live and let live," he says, his voice barely audible. "They would like...they try to surround us and do everything possible (to put us out of business). And I'm going to make it a tough as possible for them."

Carl does not intend to retire. "They're going to have to carry me out, boots first," he says.

They almost did. The last attempt to unionize Kroch's, in 1982, "really took a lot out of him," says a former employee. "He just took it so per-sonal. He lost interest in a lot of things, (including) most of the busi-ness. And he started saying, 'I could sell this thing; why do I come down every day?' He knew why. Because he doesn't have anything else. Where would he go if he didn't go to Wabash every day?"

Some have said that it is not the books but the business that is Carl Kroch's real passion. He did, in fact, agonize for many years over what to do with the business. Only in the past nine months has he finally set in motion the means by which he hopes the business will be passed along intact to the next generation, his employees.

"I'm seventy-two," he said, "I better make some decisions now." His decision was to create an Employee Stock Ownership plan, or ESOP. On January 1, 1986, the first phase of the ESOP began: Kroch sold 49.9 percent of his stock into a trustlike fund. He was paid immediately by a bank loan, which will be repaid over five years from the company's profits. When the loan is fully repaid, the stock is distributed to eligible employees. The employees themselves do not contribute anything. The remaining 50.1 percent of the stock will be sold in the same way.

When all the stock is distributed, the employees will own the company. If all goes well, that should be in ten years. Until then Kroch remains the majority stockholder.

The decision to set up the ESOP cost Kroch an estimated $5 million—the last offer from a chain competitor was said to be that much higher. But selling to a major chain would have been an admission of defeat. He doesn't like the way they do business, and he never will. By their very size, he believes, the chains unduly influence what gets published and in what quantity.

The ESOP cost him money, but it saved him two things: a tax break on the proceeds of the sale and his job. Had he sold to a chain, he would undoubtedly have replaced, as would most of his management.

After the ESOP went into effect, Kroch named McCarthy chief executive officer. McCarthy acknowledges he has a lot to learn. One of the things everyone has to learn about is how, exactly, the ESOP will work. For instance, how will the next CEO be chosen, assuming the employees own the company?

"Well, now you're over my head, I don't know that," McCarthy says. "We have a battery of attorneys, we're helping put their children through school, and they're certainly going to give us some assistance."

An even more interesting question is what happens to the 50.1 percent of stock that remains in Carl Kroch's hands if he should die before he sells it to the employees? "My lawyer is after me all the time to (do something about that)," Kroch acknowledges. "And I can't answer that. I really don't know. In my will, it sets the bank as an executor, and you know how banks mismanage things. They'd probably sell it to the highest bidder. But my lawyer says you should set up something. But you know that's one of those things that you always put off. I put off the ESOP situation for a good five years; I might have done it before. I guess if we all arranged our affairs perfectly, life would be too easy, or something like that."

Kroch insists he is not looking over McCarthy's shoulder, but there is much he must pass along in the way of financial matters—the leasing of stores, the acquiring of loans, all the details that Kroch alone has handled for the past thirty years.

A book industry executive recently had lunch with a Kroch executive. "We were talking about the ESOP," recalls the book industry executive, "and I said, 'When you go in and plot this, what kind of return-on-investment are you seeking?' And he stared at me glassy-eyed. ROI, what's that? I mean, seriously. The bottom line on this, here's a guy way up in the company, and he's never seen a financial statement. Carl has always run all that: 'Yes-I-love-you-you're-my-family-but...I keep the numbers.' "

There are some indications that Kroch is in fact yielding some control. He discovered from a book editor that McCarthy had okayed a plan to test a "rental library" for best-sellers ($1 a day, 3-day minimum), a practice that was once widespread in the industry. "I don't want to know about everything," Kroch says. "I don't feel that's too much of a major move, but I'm glad to see it because Bill is giving thought to what we might do to change things."

What if Bill and Carl disagree? "Carl is majority stockholder," McCarthy says. "He advises me. I've been made the chief executive officer. I could go against the wishes of Carl in certain things. I don't think it would be in the best interests of the company to do so."

Nor would it be in the best interests of the Cincinnati Reds to ignore their vociferous partner. When the Reds come to town, Kroch and Jet almost always go to the game. Kroch wears his red Reds sweater, red-and-white knit shirt, buttoned to his throat, red crushable rain hat and Reds watch.

Cocktails and lunch at the exclusive Stadium Club, front-row seats behind the Reds' dugout.

"Don't ask Pete Rose if he's going to retire," he instructs a reporter. "He's touchy about that." On the television in his living room Kroch has a ball autographed by Rose on the occasion of his 4,192d hit, on September 11, 1985.

Kroch exchanges brief pleasantries with Rose before the game, and waves at the Reds' first-base coach Tommy Helms. He is asked if Marge Schott, the general partner who runs the club, is coming. "She wouldn't come here," he says. "She might see me."

Kroch spent $1.2 million for his share of the Reds in 1981, when his college pal Joe Williams was the general partner. Schott took over in 1984, and in the past year the two have pursued a well-publicized feud, ever since Kroch declared that she had done a few things that were not, strictly speaking, legal.

"She is just an impossible person," he says. "There's been absolutely no communication. She never answers a letter. I have received only three letters in the two years she's been the general partner." But there may be hope. One letter, he says with a chuckle, was signed, "Love, Marge."

Meanwhile, at the game, Kroch watches intently, instructing Jet on the finer points of strategy. He applauds when a Reds batter is walked. "Walks will hurt you," he says gleefully.

Later in the same inning, when two of the Reds somehow find themselves both standing on third base at the same time, Kroch bounces to his feet and fixes the third-base area with a steady frown. The chin is set; he looks like a bulldog. Then he turns with disgust, points his index finger at his temple and says, "Dumb."

The first two innings take close to an hour. "I saw one of the fastest nine-inning games in history," he offers brightly. "Pitched by Grover Cleveland Alexander. Fifty-eight minutes. He had to get back to the bar."

Later, when the Reds take a 7–1 lead, he relaxes. He repairs to the Stadium Club for drinks after the fifth inning. He does not buy anything from vendors. He does not sing "Take Me Out to the Ballgame." He does wait until the final out before ushering his wife and friends to the exit.

The Reds win.

Just outside the ballpark, the limousine is waiting.

Annual birthday cards to Carl Kroch developed as an event for staff in all stores.

Section III

A Family Enterprise
1907–1980

Carl Kroch and his father, Adolph Kroch.

A Great Bookstore in Action

Adolph Kroch

From The Practice of Book Selection, *edited by Louis R. Wilson. Paper presented at the Library Institute at the University of Chicago, July 31-August 13, 1939. Copyright 1939 by the University of Chicago Press. All rights reserved. Reprinted by permission.*

Some three months ago I was asked to speak at the University of Chicago. The fact itself that I was to occupy a professor's chair, if even for only two hours, thrilled and flabbergasted me. I began to think about the paper the moment the subject was broached to me by Professor Carnovsky. I listened intently to his explanation of what was demanded of me and was pleased with his rather general delineation of the subject of my proposed talk. The Institute's theme was "Book Selection," but I was to speak on "A Great Bookstore in Action" or "The Autobiography of a Bookshop." Subconsciously, I thought of William Darling, that unrepentant booklover, over whose *The Private Papers of a Bankrupt Bookseller* I chuckled and was saddened as well. But here a solvent bookseller was asked to bare his soul, and I say it advisedly, because a bookseller without a soul is but a ribbon clerk. Right there and then I decided that my talk was not going to be an academic and purely objective dissertation on the science of bookselling but more of a lifestory of one who has loved books all his life and how he has handled them more or less successfully during thirty-five years of his career. In this decision to give an autobiography of a bookstore I was encouraged by Carlyle, who once said that "in those days, ten ordinary histories of Kings and Courtiers were well exchanged against the tenth part of one good history of booksellers."

Bookselling is more than the business of selling books. It is a profession that requires a thorough knowledge of books, a sympathetic understanding of the public's requirements, and a full command of modern facilities of bringing together books and the reading public on an equitable basis. It is, as Darling called it, "the very kernel of the romance of Commerce."[1] Unfortunately, the publishers have not sufficient understanding of the bookseller's problems. "To too many publishers, a good bookseller is one who buys a lot, never makes complaints, and pays his bills promptly."[2] I am quoting O.H. Cheney, whose *Economic Survey of the Book Industry*, which he undertook in

1930-31 at the request of publishers, contains a wealth of information. The Cheney report was financed by the publishers for their own, as well as the booksellers' benefit. Its sound findings were met with impressive shaking of heads on both sides of the fence dividing publishers and booksellers and promptly forgotten. This dividing-line between the two main factors of the book industry is the curse of the profession. It would seem logical that the interests of publishers as well as booksellers were alike, but in practice they are continuously at daggers' points. The bookseller's energies that should be mainly devoted to an intelligent distribution of books are squandered on meaningless squabbles with the publishers. The so-called rules and regulations, governing mutual relations of both branches, are antiquated, vague, and destructive, without regard for specific conditions and circumstances. They concern themselves with immediate results, ignoring consequences and effects on the very existence of bookstores. Although upward of 50 percent of the publishers' sales are consummated through bookstores, these outlets are being so harassed and circumscribed that the number of really fine bookshops is alarmingly declining. No other economical and more efficient method has been found to replace them.

Gladstone said that "the greatest public benefactor is the man distributing good books." Let us now look at the man and see how he does it and how he should do it.

To speak in a general way is naturally the easiest, but also the most superficial way, as it lacks the convincing power of actual proof. To speak specifically would require dealing with my own bookstores, which might create the impression of self-advertising. But, after all, I have been expressly asked to give an autobiography of a bookstore, and mine are the ones I know more intimately than anyone else's, and they are characteristic, too, of other stores in similar circumstances.

Some fifteen years ago I was asked to speak at a booksellers' convention. On rereading this paper, I found that many of my statements are as applicable to conditions today as they were then, and I will quote from them freely.

I am starting with a terrible confession. I am not what you may call a regularly trained bookseller. This handicap may encourage those enthusiastic booklovers who would like to select bookselling as a vocation. It may give them words of guidance and inspiration and some warning. In my home town, as a student, I spent most of my leisure time in reading and browsing around in bookshops. My small allowance, augmented by tutoring, I spent freely on books, gathering together an interesting library. Next to reading books and pestering booksellers with innumerable questions, the reading of book catalogs was my chief hobby. From my early youth, I felt the amenities of book-collecting, and this incomparable joy taught me the psychology of the book-buyer.

"Such a wonderful profession, that of bookselling," I thought. "All you have to do is read and caress fine books, and even if you have to part with them at times, new ones will replace the loss. You meet charming people who share your book joys, discuss with them your favorite authors, and you add to their happiness by letting them have the books they crave." Little did I know then about the trials and heartaches of bookselling. This is most fortunate, as, looking at the bright side of the calling, I failed to see the shadows. This attitude helped me in later years to overcome seemingly insurmountable difficulties. To be surrounded by books was one of my boyish dreams (I still have them), and to those boyish dreams I attribute my business success. I still share with my clients the joys they get from reading the good books which I recommend to them.

My father was a banker, and, when he tried to force me to follow his profession, I rebelled. With a bleeding heart, I sold the library I had so lovingly assembled and with the proceeds bought a third-class ticket to America. Again, books proved to be my best friends. They made it possible for me to follow instinctively the one vocation I understood; they enabled me to throw off the shackles and prejudices of the Old World and to seek here the fulfillment of my longings. Some native-born Americans do not sufficiently appreciate the thrill and exhilaration of freedom

unhampered by class prejudice. The free choice of vocation, the opportunities open alike to everyone willing to work and to struggle, are a sacred heritage we must preserve. When I came here, my first thought was of finding work among books. I heard and read wonders of this "God's country" and was convinced that people with such lofty ideals must be booklovers. I knew my native tongue, I could translate Greek into Latin, I read most of the important English books in translation, but my knowledge of colloquial English was practically nil. After a short odyssey, I found myself as a clerk in a foreign bookstore. I was happy, and even the mastery of a book-duster did not dim my enthusiasm. Later, I found that the proper wielding of a duster was the first duty of a bookseller. It helps him to keep his stock neat and clean, to keep his thoughts on books he affectionately dusts and arranges, and to remember titles through intimate association with their physical appearance. I can foretell now the efficiency of a bookselling aspirant from the way he dusts books on the first day of his apprenticeship.

In my first position I learned by contrast, always remembering to treat my prospective book purchasers in the manner I wanted to be treated myself when I was a client. I closely observed the routine and methods of the old-established business and after a while timidly approached the owner with a list of suggested improvements of service, book distribution, and method of buying. I was ridiculed by him and by the manager. They both assured me that, after twenty years of successful operation, they could dispense with advice from an inexperienced young clerk. Not many years later the old-established business failed and the manager obtained a clerical position in one of my stores.

In my position as a book clerk I began to feel terribly important. Here, I was permitted to talk to strangers, who soon became my friends, about books I loved. I sold them the books without any so-called sales effort, and they came back for more books. And why? Because I offered them something I knew, something I loved, and because I transmitted to them my honest enthusiasm. All this was unobtrusive, genuine, and not forced. Unwittingly and subconsciously, I discovered the first three fundamentals of a successful bookseller. They are (1) to know your books, (2) to become enthusiastic over them, and (3) to transmit this enthusiasm to your clients.

I spent my evenings reading. It was a grand adventure. I was making my own discoveries. There were Conrad, Hardy, Meredith, Anatole France, Whitman, Strindberg, and many other titans of literature who made my life worth living. I was filled with the glamor they instilled in me. My reading was not coordinated, mostly pell-mell, but lusty. I learned the art of rapid reading and read during the evening and late into the night, oftentimes as many as three or four books. I also tried to find out more about my own profession, studying bibliographies, books on business routine, and at last came across A. Growoll's *The Profession of Bookselling: A Handbook of Practical Hints for the Apprentice and Bookseller.* The book gave me a great many practical pointers but was too cold and uninspiring. I never could think of bookselling as a cold, matter-of-fact profession. Books to me were "choice legacies of the great, left for the enjoyment of mankind." They must not be traded in as so many pounds of flour but handled with loving care, explained and exhorted but not misrepresented. Since then I have learned that, in spite of our love for books, we must face realities and handle the profession of bookselling in a businesslike manner. The bookseller, without sacrificing his love for good books, must learn to conduct his business in competition with other businesses. A bookstore, well stocked with the best books, and staffed with intelligent bookloving assistants, is of no avail unless it is managed on sound financial principles.

Growoll's handbook for booksellers is now antiquated and should be revised and brought up to date. Ruth Brown Park's little book, *Book Shops: How to Run Them,* with an introduction and a special chapter on "Accounting" by my friend, Cedric R. Crowell, was published ten years ago. It is inspiring and informative, quite indispensable for the young bookseller, and may prove valuable to some older bookseller who was brought up in disregard of statistics and auditing figures. It certainly deserves to be brought up to date.

While most booksellers read books of every description, they habitually disregard those dealing with their own profession. Demand creates supply, and the dearth of books on bookselling is in direct proportion to the lack of interest displayed by those who continuously lament the decline of the profession. Cheney's *Survey*, which should have been read, discussed, and constantly referred to by everybody in the profession, bookseller and publisher alike, was as a publishing venture an abysmal failure. Only a fraction of the small edition was distributed and the balance of the unbound sheets destroyed. The published price was so prohibitive that I cannot help voicing a suspicion that someone intentionally tried to suppress Cheney's findings.

Let me now go back to our young book clerk. After three years of clerical work, I became restless and dissatisfied. The sphere of my activities became too cramped for my vision, and I felt that the time had come for "love to conquer all." In this case it was my love for books that was to conquer my very limited capital. I resigned my position and began to look around for a store in which I was to prove the soundness of my bookselling principles. I found a small store on a side street with a frontage of twenty feet and a depth of about sixty feet. Simple shelves and tables were

The original A. Kroch & Company German bookstore, located on Monroe Street, drawn by Phil Austin, 1907.

installed. For stock I gathered together books that I knew, not merely a haphazard selection, but only such books as appealed personally to my literary taste and with the unfaltering conviction that those books would appeal to my clients. The next task was my window. I realized from the start that the window was to bare my business soul, trying to embrace all good books; and, accordingly, I arranged my first window display. I was so proud of my books that everyone was to receive a prominent position; the more I loved the book, the more prominent the location. So the window became my real business card, the expression of my individuality. The public noticed the expression, caught the spirit, and began to come in. I talked to them about my books; it was I who led the conversation. I spoke to them about the subject I knew best, about the books I loved, and evoked in them the desire to know more about the books. Here is the fourth fundamental rule for the successful bookseller: to make the public want the books you want them to read.

This power to mold the mental requirements of the public must be wielded with tact, discretion, and absolute honesty. I succeeded in impressing my clients with the fact that reading good books is not only a pastime, a sport of a thousand thrills, but also a profitable occupation, as it elevates the reader above the dull crowd, offers him the best topic of conversation among intelligent people, and entitles him to the privileges of the only true aristocracy—the aristocracy of mind. He can also share this distinction and pay the finest compliments to his friends' intellects by giving them books as gifts for any and every occasion. To be met in a bookstore known for its good books is really a worthwhile distinction.

The mentally alert bookseller has a further opportunity, if not duty, to improve the taste of the reading public. When a genuine effort is made to impress the reader with the beauties of literature in contrast to the shallowness of near-literature, it will usually meet with success. It has to be done gradually, tactfully, and persistently. The bookseller's own enthusiasm for literature and his belief that the public is susceptible to good books are his best assistants. Genuine gratitude and affection of attached active buyers will be the bookseller's ample reward.

After several years, I moved to larger quarters on Michigan Avenue, which was then not the prominent thoroughfare it is today. The store soon became known as "the meeting place of intellectual Chicago." Literary critics and young authors met here almost daily-the explosively enthusiastic Burton Rascoe; the staid, reserved, and learned Harry Hansen; the delicately effusive Johnnie Weaver; Vincent Starrett; the grand siegneur of letters; Gene Markey, the impressive; Sterling North, who promised much and gave us even more; John Drury, the gourmandizing litterateur; Ben Hecht, the budding cynic; and many, many others. This is what Harry Hansen in his *Midwest Portraits* has to say about Kroch's of that period (1923):

> But it is the individual bookseller who has been the greatest force in shaping the reading taste of Chicago. Can a bookseller actually influence the taste of a community? Most assuredly he can when he brings imagination into his business methods and becomes more than a mere vendor of books. And singularly enough, the moment he does so, his material returns increase and prosperity stares him in the face. Bookselling is an occupation to which men may bring high hopes and enthusiasms and once an audience is gained, they may realize in it some of their finest aspirations. The book buyer is pliable; he can be led meekly

into new pastures or absolutely discouraged in his reading; once his interest is obtained he becomes a firm friend. In Chicago this has been proved conclusively by the success of A. Kroch. His store, which grew from a little hole in the wall on Monroe Street ten years ago to its present proportions, holds an enviable place in the minds of the booksellers of America. When its profits are discussed, booksellers invariably try to explain its success in terms of its location (on Michigan Avenue, the broad highway of Chicago), its owner's foresight in buying and his ability to keep his stock moving. But an actual study of his methods would show that his influence as a cultural factor has been mainly responsible for his position. To Mr. Kroch, books are not like so many crates of eggs or sacks of coffee—they are friends, and in the quiet of his home he reads as diligently as a reviewer. He then studies the men and the women who enter his store and is able to lead them to books that they will enjoy. The virtue of knowing good books and then finding readers for them is similar to that which makes good editors, good architects, good musicians; it can be expressed in terms of salesmanship or inspiration. Today, Mr. Kroch touches hands with an innumerable company of readers, many of whom ascribe their reading habit to his personal interest in them. What in an ordinary inventory of a business house would be described as good will, may be translated here in the terms "confidence in his judgement," and this is the biggest asset in the Kroch organization.[3]

Young authors were excitedly discussed, praised to dizzy heights, and their books sold in unprecedented quantities. Some are now almost forgotten, but many reached the ranks of best-sellerdom. James Branch Cabell was discovered here and preached persistently to all America; Remy de Gourmont served up to literary gourmets; Willa Cather hailed as one of America's greatest; Edna St. Vincent Millay first recognized; James Stephens chuckled over and forced down the throats; Logan Pearsall Smith reverently eulogized. There was a tension, an exhilarating enthusiasm, that inoculated all who came to Kroch's, giving it an atmosphere of unassuming culture.

But, with all the apparent success, I was not quite satisfied. I realized that my personal service appealed to a limited number of readers, that there were thousands of potential readers whom I could not hope to reach with my limited resources. I began to dream of a really great bookshop representative of the great literary output of awakening America. I had definite ideas of what such an ideal bookstore should look like, its physical greatness, its encompassing stock of books embracing all fields of literature, its trained, well-informed staff of expert book people, and its great facilities of offering complete book service in all its ramifications. Slowly the dream became a reality, and after years of preparation a really imposing bookstore in the present location was established. A complete remodeling of the available large space of three floors, comprising over twenty thousand square feet, was intrusted to experienced architects. Store fixtures were especially designed to hold and display an adequately representative stock of books of all publishers, popular as well as scientific. In addition to the departments such as those of technical books, art books, business books, circulation library, art galleries, old and rare books, foreign books, and juvenile books had to be organized. A mail-order department had to be equipped with addressographs, mimeographing machines, and other facilities for producing circulars, letters, and announcements. An experienced advertising man had to be charged with the duties of coordinating newspaper and direct-mail publicity. An efficient bookkeeping, auditing, and statistical department was intrusted with the task of keeping a vigilant eye over the financial structure of the organization.

Ten thousand announcements to regular clients and new prospective book-buyers were posted, and the hundred and fifty lineal feet of windows were artistically decorated with books to warm any bibliophile's heart and to untie the purse strings of a Scotsman. Everything was ready for the grand opening day! And it came! The weatherman reports that a snowstorm of unheard-of severity struck Chicago on that memorable day in December. Heavy snow began to fall early in the morning, and, by the time set for the official opening, all transportation facilities were crippled, the streets became impassable, and here I was waiting at the Cathedral of Muses! Some reckless bibliomaniacs risked their limbs and made their appearance, and how I appreciated those few who, undeterred by the infuriated elements, came to celebrate with me this new era in modern bookselling. At last the storm subsided. The streets were cleared, and I settled down to routine action in a Great Bookstore.

The component elements of a great bookstore are: (1) stock, (2) personnel, (3) publicity, and (4) budgeting. Each one must be applied to achieve the maximum in sales.

The generally accepted method of purchasing books is through publishers' representatives or salesman who call on the bookseller from two to eight times a year and show him their new titles. Soon after I had established my business I discovered a new art-"the gentle art of making enemies" among those representatives who thought they knew more about my wants than I myself and were anxious to find a resting place for their would-be remainders. But these shortsighted salesmen are, fortunately, in the minority. The more farsighted salesman endeavor to appreciate the bookseller's position and try honestly to answer questions to the best of their ability. They understand that my mode of buying is not a matter of favoritism but merely a sincere desire to convince myself whether I am able to sell the book in question and particularly whether I can find the reader to fit the book and to what extent. A publisher's representative may show from ten to forty books at the time of the appointment. In many instances he has merely samples of the jackets, a few printed pages, and a stereotype sales talk. He but seldom has had the occasion to read the book in advance, and the sorely-pressed-for-time buyer only half-listens to the talk of the salesman. The bookseller's attitude is a classical "no," and in two cases out of ten he is right. Multiply this procedure by about twenty of the more important publishers and some thirty of the lesser lights, and you have the tragic picture of how America's literary output is presented to the bookseller. We all know that this method is wasteful, unreliable, and entirely unsatisfactory. The publisher occasionally tries to overcome it by sending out advance copies of his more important books, which is a step in the right direction. But you must consider that an important bookseller receives from ten to twenty-five and more advance copies a week, and, although he distributes the books among his assistants, it is quite difficult to read them all. The remedy is fewer and better books. There are various reasons, of course, which a publisher has for publishing so many books:

1. His overhead charges require the publication of a certain number of books.

2. His author, whose previous book sold in satisfactory quantities, may again write a best-seller, and he does not dare to offend him by refusing to publish his book, which he knows to be poor, because another publisher will bring it out and wean the author away from him.

3. He does not trust his own judgment and, being in a highly speculative business, hopes against hope that the book will sell in spite of its poor quality.

4. The publisher was ill-advised by an incompetent reader.

5. Another publisher was successful with a similar subject, so why not try to emulate him.

6. The public should be interested in a particular pertinent subject.

There is a vast difference, however, between what the public is interested in and what it should be interested in. There are, no doubt, some additional reasons why so many poor books are published, but those enumerated are sufficient to consider the situation and try to remedy it. I am meeting it by never buying an appreciable quantity of a book without having read it myself or its having been read by one or more competent assistants. When buying new books, I consult with my staff and tabulate their reactions.

When in doubt, I reserve the return privilege, as we will never willingly sell a book to the public which we believe to be poor, and extend an unconditional exchange privilege on all books we are selling. Large special works are bought only when we can visualize a definite market. Through reading foreign, and particularly English, literary journals, I keep informed on new books before they have reached the American market and have a standing order with my British agents for sample copies of all the new important books.

I am particularly suspicious of new books of successful authors which closely follow their previous success. They are in quality and sales appeal usually inferior to their predecessors. Books by new authors are read in advance with sympathetic reserve. I am a sleuth, always suspecting the quality of the book, but forever hoping to discover a great book. When the hunt is successful, I am thrilled, exuberantly happy, and ready to go to bat against all odds, but I must be convinced of the high quality of the book. A good book must be readable; it must thrill you; it must hold you; it must make you forget time and weather; it must force you to shout from the housetops: "Here is a book!" and, whenever I discover such a book, I am fully compensated for frequent disappointments.

But how about the public? I often wonder why books are still being read. With thousands of unsuitable, unworthy books foisted upon them, the readers become discouraged, skeptical, and prefer to visit the cinema or listen to the radio. I do not blame them. But give me the people to visit my store, let me talk to them, let me discover their mental makeup, and I will prove to them the joy of reading. All this can be done more effectively with fewer and better books.

Of late, some publishers, realizing the economic and emotional waste of overproduction, have been more rigid in their selection of books. Their lists of books are smaller, their selection more careful, their advertising programs better planned. They aim to give the bookseller, well in advance, incisive information about their publishing programs, with the result that their imprint as publishers is synonymous with literary quality and undeceptive salability and is fully recognized and esteemed as such. Their outstanding financial success is further proof of the soundness of such procedure.

The bookstore's greatest asset is its personnel. What are the qualifications of the staff and where are its members to be drawn from? That a bookseller is born and not made is not exactly true, but it has a grain of reason. He must have a solid background of good schooling. He must know the fundamentals of good literature. He must have a pleasing personality without being an Adonis; he must have a pleasant and convincing manner of speaking; he must tact and an understanding of human nature; he must pay attention to details; he must be industrious, persevering, venturesome, liberal, kindhearted, but, above all, he must be enthusiastic. In speaking of "him" I naturally also refer to "her," as women are admirably suited to this profession and more than one-half of my staff consists of women. But where to get these ideal creatures? I do not expect all the enumerated qualifications in all the individuals who work for me, but they must possess the majority of virtues; otherwise let them become ribbon clerks. They, themselves, must have experienced the joy of reading. They must be capable of keeping up the undying fire of enthusiasm. They must understand that the client's interests, theirs, and mine are alike. Honest, cheerful service must be their watchword, expressed in harmonious team work. But here I must touch upon a sore spot in our profession. The material to draw upon is quite limited and inadequate. To remedy it, there should be established full-time bookselling schools and not merely evening classes. Possibly some connection with library schools would prove satisfactory. I would prescribe a two-year university course, majoring in literature, one year of business training, and one year's apprenticeship in a well-conducted bookstore. A final examination before the board of the Booksellers Association would entitle the successful candidate to a degree of a B.C.(Book Counselor). With such material, we could approach a plan of the utmost importance to the welfare of our profession-a great national

booksellers' campaign of which I will speak later.

At the present time I select my assistants in a somewhat haphazard way, and, after they have displayed an aptitude for the profession, I train them in the art of bookselling. I prefer college boys and girls who worked through their school years. I choose teachers for certain departments, but usually our customary business hours seem too long for them. I accept librarians, but must break them of the habit of giving something for nothing, and instill in them the understanding that in a bookstore books are to be sold and not loaned out free of charge! Any intelligent young person who has an understanding for literature and a deep-seated willingness to work hard is fitted for the profession of bookselling. The rewards are comparable to those in other professions, and the satisfaction is greater. But, before the promising field of bookselling can attract exceptional material, we must clean house and inaugurate certain reforms and improvements, of which I will speak later.

A book on the bookseller's shelves is of no use to anybody. His methods of placing them with the ultimate buyer represent the real objective of bookselling. He does it (1) through personal recommendations, (2) through newspaper advertisements, (3) through letters and circulars, (4) through telephone solicitations, and (5) through personal calls. Personal contact between bookseller and reader is the most satisfactory method of

Massive displays and theme treatments characterize Kroch's & Brentano's windows.

book distribution, but it presupposes that the reader, by visiting the bookshop, will expose himself to the bookseller's influence. The latter has various methods of attracting the reader. His window displays are his silent, but no less effective, salesmen. A window not only is the store's visiting card but is also a vivid reflection of literary trends and expresses the political tendencies then prevailing in the country. The sorrowful book windows in totalitarian states are best proofs of this contention.

There are two major methods of window displays: the mass display of one single title to center the onlooker's attention on one book which enjoys particular popularity at the time and a great diversification of a large variety of titles. I prefer combining both features, by prominently displaying several titles in reasonable quantities, but also showing many other books

arranged according to subjects. Anyone studying my windows can obtain a graphic impression of the literature output over a period of several months. Harmony of colors, association of ideas, and pleasing arrangements are the compelling features that will transform a window-shopper into a visitor. When he enters the store and evinces an interest in a book, it is up to the bookseller to give him a reliable information based on actual knowledge and not meaningless generalities. The book-buyer generally has but a vague idea of what he wants; therefore, if the bookseller patiently and tactfully demonstrates to him his thorough familiarity with the subject under discussion, then he is of real service.

No reader can expect a bookseller to know intimately every book on his shelves, but he should be able to obtain sufficient information to form his own opinion about the book, such as the subject it treats of, the style of the writing, and the general standing of the author. The books the book-seller has read are, of course, easiest sold, and this is the principal reason why those of my assistants who are omnivorous, critical readers are the most successful salesmen. Through the informative, tactful advice they give to grateful readers, they develop a bond of lasting friendships which are the bookseller's greatest assets. On the other hand, many a potential book-buyer has been lost forever by receiving misleading information about the books he bought. Frequent disap-pointments are so discouraging to him that he eventually gets the impression that reading books is a dull and use-less waste of time. There is no man or woman who, when properly guided, could not be shown the joys and the satisfaction that can be derived from properly selected reading. Once those first formative steps have been guided in the right direction, he will explore by himself the various ramifications of the world of books; he will attain con-fidence in his own judgment, but will continue to seek poignant advice from his bookseller friend.

We know, of course, that one of the really great objectives of schools and colleges is to instill in young minds the joys, and not merely the duties, of reading. Unfortunately, this great opportunity is oftentimes sorely neglected. This is why bookselling is,

in my opinion, not merely a business to sell books but a serious responsibil-ity for molding the minds of a nation. I am grateful to Hendrik Willem Van Loon for his understanding tribute to my profession in his *R. v. R.* He says:

> For the book-seller is a man who carries a magic key in his pocket, and if you are able to gain his good will, unlock such wondrous treasure-chests for you that you never need experience another dull moment as long as you live. The bookseller, of course, is in business to make a living and he will charge you for his services, as is not only his good right, but also his duty. But listen, O my son, and treat thy book-seller as thy best friend and he will repay thee beyond the miser's fondest dreams of un-earned increment.[4]

And David Garnett, once a book-seller, in his little essay, *Never Be a Bookseller*, speaks of him as:

> the kindest-hearted man alive and extraordinarily long-suffering. He works hard for small returns, he usually spends half his time in giving free advice to everyone in his town, he does all the hard work in the book trade. He sells the books I write and he keeps on selling them. When I think of what that means I thank my stars that now I only have to write them.[5]

But he ends by saying, "Yet sometimes I wish I were back in the shop. It was a great game." Such are the trials, tribulations, and rewards of bookselling.

Some of the larger newspapers have more or less important sections devoted to book-reviewing. Some book reviews are thoroughly informative; others startle the reader with the brillance of the reviewer's mind, his encompassing knowledge of literature, but fail to convey the really characteristic points of the book under review. The book-reviewer justly resents the implication that his objective is to sell books. It is, of course, his duty to criticize books and to express his frank opinion of their literary, informative, or entertaining quality; but a real test of a favorable review is the public's response. If the reviewer unintentionally succeeds in evoking in a number of people the desire to read the book and to back up his judgment with time and money, then the review has accomplished a real service to the reader and to literature in general. The bookseller accepts his valuable judgment and follows him with appreciative gratitude. Their objective, to disseminate knowledge of good books, is then quite mutual.

Publishers attempt to publicize books by scattered advertisements in newspapers, magazines, and circulars. With very few exceptions, these efforts are meaningless, inadequate, and ineffective. When a manufacturer of toothpaste decides on a selling campaign, he selects an advertising expert who studies the product, examines all its characteristics, obvious as well as imaginary, and propounds them to the public through countless repetition, using a formidable amount of advertising space. His appeal is directed to about 95 percent of the readers who are potential toothpaste purchasers. Books appeal to possibly 10 percent of newspaper readers, but the advertising rate on books slightly differs from that of toothpaste. The publisher cannot possibly spend an adequate amount to advertise his books. He appropriates a certain modest sum for advertising largely to satisfy the author, to still the booksellers' clamoring, and to justify the book page. His appropriation is thinly spread over dozens of titles, with very insignificant returns for his expenditure. His best-seller is advertised more prominently to keep that particular title in the public's mind. In my opinion, publishers should advertise primarily the joys of reading to make the public more generally book conscious; then, the pleasure of owning books; and finally, they should advertise bookstores, where books and information about them can be readily obtained, the expense of the latter to be shared by publisher and bookseller. Expert advertising men should be intrusted with such a well-planned, persistent campaign that is bound to give them healthy outlets for the sale of their books. When individual titles are advertised, they must give characteristics that will inform and not generalize through the use of meaningless superlatives. The method which I find best for testing an advertisement or a circular is the substituting of one title for another, and, if the description fits both titles, then it is neither characteristic nor informative, but misleading.

The greatest amount of my energy is spent on efforts to bring more people to the store. In this I am constantly hampered by the publishers themselves. They not only attempt to sell directly to the public, thus eliminating the bookseller, but fall for almost any scheme to achieve wider distribution to the exclusion of the bookseller. Tempted by immediate profits, they have contributed to the growth of book clubs, which, by their tens of thousands of members, have weaned the public from the habit of regularly visiting bookstores. The book club's main appeal is the price differential, and since their actual cost of books represents but a fraction of that of a bookseller, their competition is destructive to the bookstore.

Some time ago I inaugurated a book-a-month service, selecting, in contrast to present book clubs, a book each month which suited the individual taste of the reader whom I knew personally. But since I am compelled to pay the regular publishers' prices, which obviates cutting list prices and spending enormous sums on advertising "bargains," I find that I cannot compete with the book clubs on a mere price basis. If the reader will only realize that by receiving fewer books, selected to his personal taste, rather than having many books foisted upon him in a mass selection, he will be better served by the bookstore!

While the publishers may gain some new readers by encouraging book clubs, they lose thousands of habitual book-buyers. Book clubs, while helping so-called "best-sellers" to reach dizzy heights, overshadow many a good book, since there are not enough visitors to bookstores to whose attention the book can be brought by the bookseller. Furthermore, mass selection by book clubs does not tend to develop real booklovers. It is an almost unbelievable fact that efficient book outlets, vital to the publishers' independent existence, are being destroyed by the publishers themselves.

Newspapers should also support the united efforts to convey the joys of reading and owning books by adequate articles. Their really informative book page would attract quality circulation and their well-thought-out service to the reading public would enlarge their scope of influence. During my bookselling career I have expended large amounts of money on full page and smaller advertisements, but this has been only a small and inadequate effort. Only through united action can the public be awakened to the important role books should and could play in our pursuit of happiness through selective reading.

In addition to newspaper advertising, I mail out large quantities of a monthly book bulletin aptly named by me, *Rest and Read*, which aims to keep my clients informed on new books. Outstanding books of the month are also covered by special circulars and personal letters. We write hundreds of individual letters to tabulated lists of readers, offering books that fit their individual preferences. Occasionally we prepare the field for important books months in advance, with gratifying results. For Simon & Schuster's *A Treasury of Art Masterpieces*, by Thomas Craven, a really monumental publishing undertaking, we have booked over eight hundred orders, although the book was not to be published for another two months. The combination of the publisher's well thought-out brochure on the book, which they supplied to us, and our enthusiastic efforts, produced these gratifying returns.

When a book is, in my opinion, especially deserving, I use a combined barrage of methods to exploit all sales possibilities. It becomes a matter of professional duty to place a large number with the reading public. Costs of distribution are then obviously disregarded, and oftentimes I have had the satisfaction of creating national demand. It is occasionally a long and uphill strife, but the thrill and satisfaction of sharing such joys of discovery with many people, far beyond the sphere of my own influence, are a great reward for efforts expended. I remember once of having become enamored with a book that had everything against it: a bad title, an unpopular subject, an unknown author, and still I believed it to be a great book. When all my efforts failed, I prepared, in desperation, a short letter urging my clients to read the book on my sole recommendation, offering to send it on inspection and promising to refund double the amount of the cost of the book. I was ready to repay $2.50 for the book and $2.50 for the time wasted in reading it. The reader was to be the sole judge. This startling offer broke the ice of resistance. I sold several thousand copies, and only two copies were returned! The book eventually became very popular.

Each special department, such as art, technical, etc., sends out monthly, descriptive lists of new books in its field. My list of clients is tabulated according to subjects, author preferences, and hobbies. The more obscure the subject, the greater the percentage the percentual return, which proves the individual's appreciation of a personalized service.

Each day's work starts with a short discussion of new books published that day, conducted by myself and my buyer. The soul of each book is carefully dissected and its sales possibilities analyzed, with each salesman having an equal voice in the discussion. Then, the real task of matching the books with prospective readers commences and the fun of bookselling fills a busy day. No book is buried on the shelves to await a caller without first being thoroughly exploited. Each department is charged with the responsibility of matching each new book with its logical reader. The match must be perfect, otherwise the book will be promptly returned by the purchaser.

Libraries constitute one of the most important book markets. They spend approximately twelve million dollars yearly on books. Of this amount, according to Cheney, only about 40 percent is spent through local bookstores, but I believe even this low estimate is growing steadily smaller. Library purchases enable the bookseller to obtain better terms from the publishers, to employ larger staffs, to carry more varied stocks, to be in closer touch with the literary output, and to be held in greater esteem by the publishers. All this, in turn, results in better service to the public. The librarian, in most cases supported by public funds, should have this mutual obligation at heart and give preference to the bookstore equipped to handle library orders, instead of purchasing books from the jobber or directly from the publisher. He should not attempt to drive a hard bargain by demanding an exorbitant discount, which would make it impossible for the bookseller to derive a modest legitimate profit. The librarian who regularly visits the bookstore keeps in closer touch with literary trends, and, by examining the books, avoids costly mistakes, which are bound to occur when orders are prepared from cold lists. It greatly simplifies his task and enables him to devote more time to the public. Where satisfactory service relationship between the library and the bookstore has been built up over a period of years, this should not be disturbed by outside offers of higher discounts.

Librarians from surrounding small towns, with inadequate or nonexisting bookstore facilities, regularly visit my bookstore. They obtain firsthand information, discuss literary qualities, trends, and editions, and I gain from their animated conversations that they hugely enjoy this contact with the bookstore. Some college librarians occasionally arrange excursions to my shop, bringing as many as ten to fifty students. This gives me the opportunity to talk to young people about the joys of reading. I can explain the beauties of fine printing by showing them, for instance, a noble page from the Gutenberg Bible, as compared with that other example of fine printing, the Kelmscott Chaucer. I am able to tell them of the various editions, amusing them with quaint histories of some books, and explain to them the work of master-binders. In parting, they usually tell me that they never had suspected so much romance in books! The seeds of a bibliophile are thus implanted in receptive minds, to make their lives richer and fuller. Their questions about books, at first timid but later on enthusiastic, are a joy to the heart of a book vendor. He forgets commerce and feels that what has been created in the sweat of genius should be fanned into a mighty fire, to light the sinister darkness of ignorance and intolerance.

The bookseller and the librarian should work hand in hand supplementing their service to the reading public. Every larger town where this relationship exists usually can boast of a well-conducted bookstore. In contrast to this, I know of a number of bookstores which have declined or have entirely disappeared, after the library connection was taken away from them.

While the bookseller's labor is that of love for the elusive term known as "literature," he must be a practical merchant in order to survive. I solved the problem by remembering that the average dollar I receive for selling a book must be spent by me as follows: 65 cents for the book, 16 cents for salaries, 6 cents, for rent, 3 cents for advertising, 2 cents for freight, 1 cent for markdowns, and 5 cents for general expenses, such as light, telephone, supplies, social security, etc. This leaves a profit of 2 cents. Most of these enumerated expenses are fixed, and the slightest unbalancing of the budget upsets the cart and swallows up my profit, turning it oftentimes into loss.

Library business must be considered separately from the regular business. A maximum library discount of 25 percent on regular list-price books helps to carry the fixed charges and may result in a maximum profit of 1 percent. A larger library discount is decidedly suicidal. This is a fact supported by the experience of solvent booksellers and substantiated by Cheney's findings. I welcome the opinion of any librarian who could challenge and disprove this statement.

There are about 1.6 million retail stores in the United States and, of these, only about four thousand are retail book outlets. These include about twenty-five hundred insignificant outlets hardly deserving the designation of bookstores; another thousand do not carry representative stocks of books, so that there are about five hundred book departments or bookstores more or less competent to care for the book needs of 130 million Americans! This is a very sorrowful picture, and, if you realize that only one-fifth of one cent of the American dollar is spent on books, while about nineteen cents is spent on automobiles and one and a half cents on candy, you will have a conception of both the plight and the possibilities of bookselling.

In the narrow space of time at my disposal, I have attempted to analyze the reasons for the decline of bookstores and have suggested some possible remedies. In conclusion, the following plan summarizes my experience gained over a period of more than thirty years of active bookselling. It is presented without rancor or bitterness, solely in the hope that it may awaken America's responsibilities toward a profession that, when properly fostered, can add untold riches to the intellectual wealth and happiness of a nation.

Publishers, as well as booksellers, must fully realize the shortcomings of the entire industry. Let them appoint a committee of at least five members, consisting of one publisher, one bookseller, one author, one librarian, and, as chairman, a business executive with accounting experience. This committee, whose members would be appointed for two years and be well compensated, should study data assembled by Cheney, the American Booksellers Association, and the American Publishers Association, and should be given power to act and to put their rulings into practice. Duties and privileges of publishers should be defined, booksellers should be classified in accordance with their capacity to serve, training of the personnel qualified, markets analyzed, localities that need book outlets investigated, relations of libraries to bookstores studied, advertising policies defined, methods of accounting standardized, duties and spheres of action of wholesale houses investigated, regional depositories considered, "reminder" problems stabilized, and bookselling manuals prepared. The scope is very large, but, once the work is started in a spirit of mutual cooperation, a definite program would be mapped out and each step thoroughly prepared. But it is absolutely essential that the committee be vested with some power of instigating the practical application of its rulings, as otherwise its findings would have no greater significance than the Cheney report.

I may be accused of being an impractical visionary who suggests the impossible. I am fully aware of the great difficulties, but my entire bookselling career is proof of my clear understanding of its problem. My suggestion to examine and analyze bookselling is born out of a real devotion to an ennobling profession that I see failing in its duties and opportunities to serve. Many a great industry and many a vocation has gone through a period of disintegration and has been saved by courageous action of far-seeing members who had the daring to see faults and the resoluteness, fearlessness, and vision to meet the problems, to cope with them and to solve them.

I no doubt have gone beyond the scope of my paper, and yet I have only touched upon subjects that require vastly greater elaboration. As I analyzed, studied, and investigated this "Autobiography of a Bookstore" through a process of self-analysis, I had to recognize the various circumstances that have hampered my colleagues and myself in the fulfilment of rightful duties of a noble profession. Let bookselling cease to be, as Madge Jenison called it, "a great lost cause." Let both the bookseller as well as the publisher become impressed with the seriousness and great responsibility of their vocation. Let the public become conscious of the fact that the bookseller is the logical mental adviser, that he is the one who awakens the mind of the child, molds the thought of youth, and broadens the view of the mature man or woman. Let us accept the new definition of a bookseller-that of a practical idealist.

1. [William Y. Darling], *The Private Papers of a Bankrupt Bookseller* (London: Oliver & Boyd, 1932), p. 40.

2. O.H. Cheney, *Economic Survey of the Book Industry, 1930–31: Final Report* (New York: National Association of Book Publishers, 1931), p. 258.

3. Harry Hansen, *Midwest Portraits: A Book of Memories and Friendships* (New York: Harcourt, Brace & Co., 1923), pp. 196–97.

4. Hendrik W. Van Loon, *R.v.R.: The Life & Times of Rembrandt van Rijn* (New York: Literary Guild, 1930), p. 447.

5. David Garnett, *Never Be a Bookseller* (New York: A.A. Knopf, 1929), p. xiv.

A Bookseller's Responsibilities

Carl A. Kroch

My interpretation of the purpose of
this colloquium is to define the
responsibilities of parties involved in
the book distribution process to each
other. As a bookseller I hope to
explain my relationship with publishers, authors, and, of course, with the
book-reading public. Before I do so I
will digress and give a short resume of
my career as a bookseller and the
many changes I have seen in the forty-
five years I have devoted to the
wonderful profession.

On April 9, 1935, I formally
became a bookseller. I say "formally"
because I was a bookseller since the
dawn of my consciousness. My father
had opened his own bookstore in 1907
and from early childhood I heard
discussions of the trials and tribulations of bookselling. I regularly met
authors, publishers, and other booksellers in our family home. I graduated from Cornell University in
February 1935 and, after a few months
of vacationing, joined my father on
that fateful April date. I had worked

for Dad after school and during
vacations but now, at last, I would be a
full-fledged member of that fraternity
of which I had heard so much.

At that time the Kroch bookselling
empire consisted of a large Kroch's
store on Michigan Avenue in Chicago,
where I started my career, a small
branch on La Salle Street, Chicago's
financial center, and the Chicago
Brentano's store which had been
bought by my father when that
venerable chain went bankrupt in
1933. I started out as a very junior
salesman. My main duties for the first
few months were dusting and alpha-
betizing shelves and shelves of books,
under the watchful eye of my father.
He was not only the owner but also
buyer, general manager, head salesman, personnel director, advertising
manager, and copywriter, and he also
performed a thousand other duties.

Kroch's on Michigan Avenue,
which Dad grandly called "the
Meeting Place of Intellectual Chicago,"
was a good-sized store with a sales
volume of about three hundred
thousand dollars per year. When you
consider that novels sold then for two
dollars or at the most two dollars and
a half, that volume would translate
into about $1 million today. It was a

complete bookstore with a trade department, children's books, an excellent art department, well-stocked technical, scientific, and business book departments, and a representative foreign book department. We also had an old and rare book department featuring books in leather bindings and a good selection of not-too-expensive rare books.

Dad was a super salesman. He was devoted to the treasure he was selling, and he was also that rarity among idealists, a good practical businessman. Just two examples will demonstrate that practicality. When the Great Depression of the thirties finally reached the book business in 1931, Dad was saddled with an annual rent for the Michigan Avenue store of fifty thousand dollars which the business could not afford to pay. He approached the landlord and suggested that the lease be cancelled and a percentage lease, in which the amount paid is based on the volume of sales, be substituted for it. It is hard to believe that a landlord would cancel a good lease, but those were desperate times, and Dad was very persuasive. The landlord consented to the new lease. The percentage decided on was 6 percent, which even today is the recognized figure for rent in bookstores.

Something else that is difficult for younger booksellers to realize is that books were sold on an outright and not a returnable basis you bought a book and couldn't sell it you were stuck with it. Dad, out of necessity,

made a change in this method of buying. The necessity was the fact that he did not have sufficient capital to stock the stores. When buying new books he would tell the salesman, "I'll take twenty-five copies—ten outright and fifteen for display." The "display" meant, of course, on consignment and these books were returnable. Thus, necessity was the beginning of the purchase of books on a returnable basis.

Our normal workweek was a six-day fifty-four-hour week, and once a week after store hours Dad would call a meeting of the sales staff to discuss any unusual problems and hear their comments on new books that they particularly liked. From the very first of these meetings I learned the reason for Dad's success as a salesman—enthusiasm. He stressed that knowledge of your product or subject was essential, but without enthusiasm you could not transmit that knowledge to prospective buyers. I, too, feel that enthusiasm is all-important and I stress this at our staff meetings. With a present-day staff of over seven hundred, I don't do any selling to individual customers but try to do it on a mass, but still personal, basis. For seven years I wrote a "Tending Store" column in a weekly advertisement we ran in the book section of the *Chicago Tribune*, and it is still running in *Chicago* magazine. "Tending Store" is a conversational column about books and my personal experiences in the business.

It was our good fortune to have as manager of the Brentano's store W. W.

Clear signage, well-lit displays and inviting merchandising techniques make Kroch's & Brentano's accessible to all customers.

Goodpasture, known to one and all in the trade as "Goody," and he made a number of important contributions to bookselling as we know it today. For example, it was he who persuaded publishers to sell backlist titles on a dating basis so that we could buy and receive those titles in summer and pay for them in January. Goody also decided by 1952, when we combined Kroch's & Brentano's in the "World's Largest Bookstore," that there was a future in selling paperback books, and we opened a Super Book Mart featuring an unheard-of selection of fifteen thousand paperback titles. In a 1953 issue of *Life* magazine a picture of our Super Book Mart appeared with the caption: "New way to sell books was supermarket style—as inaugurated by Kroch's & Brentano's in Chicago."

In planning the Super Book Mart, Goody and I realized that books could not be effectively displayed on shelves with the spine out. Publishers spent considerable amounts of money on book jackets and we were hiding these jackets by displaying only the spine. We adapted these fixtures used in the greeting card industry and designed curved racks with shelves tilted so that we could display the full covers of books. These racks have become standard for displaying books. We also fitted the book racks with canopy lights and increased the lighting level throughout the store, a favor to customers who had come to expect darker, less pleasant surroundings in bookstores of the past.

Recently we have developed the "full-service" bookstore concept, following the example of the banking industry, which has advertised the idea so successfully. The term "The Full Service Bookstores" has been registered in the United States Patent Office and may be used exclusively by Kroch's & Brentano's. Here is our Full Service creed as I hope we practice it in our eighteen stores:

1. A convenient location.
2. An attractive decor with fixtures specifically designed to display books, and good lighting to make browsing more pleasant.
3. A well-selected inventory of books on all subjects in both hardbound and paperback editions. To include such rather specialized fields as technical, scientific and business, art, and the social sciences. To carry not only the latest books on all subjects but also standard backlist titles.
4. A sales staff able to counsel customers in the selection of books on any subject.
5. Regular mailings of catalogs to customers advising them of important new books on a variety of subjects.
6. Charge accounts for those customers desiring credit.
7. Delivery of merchandise purchased.
8. Full return privilege (refund of purchase price) on any book not entirely satisfactory.
9. A willingness to take special orders for books not in stock and procedures to make prompt delivery of such special orders.
10. Mail and telephone order departments staffed by experienced and

competent employees for customers wishing to order in this manner.

I hope that I have not lost my audience with this lengthy introduction. Now I would like to discuss my feelings about our relationship with our customers. First, a bookseller must be a competent businessman. Bookselling requires all the systems and controls that any retail business must have if it is to operate successfully. And if a bookseller is not successful he cannot serve his customers. Equally important is a love of books and the passionate feeling that they deserve to be disseminated as widely as possible. This enthusiasm for books is necessary not only in the small personal bookstore but also in large organizations such as Kroch's & Bretano's. Many of our salespeople already share our love of books when they come to K & B; and we encourage them to continue learning about books and express their enthusiasm to their customers. When it comes time to fill supervisory and management positions, these eager, enthusiastic, knowledgeable people make excellent candidates. I think it is a telling fact about K & B that our entire staff-from the top down-has been promoted from within.

Next, a bookseller must attempt to provide his customers with a selection of merchandise that will fill any reasonable request. I am speaking not just of new books, but particularly of backlist. At K & B we try to have an assortment of books on every conceivable subject. Our aim is to carry any

This Month at Kroch's, *1950. Kroch's & Brentano's pioneered catalogs and direct mail techniques to sell books.*

title for which we believe there is a probable sale of at least three copies per year. If that cannot be expected, we do not stock it but we will special order it.

Third, and vital for a successful bookseller, is the refusal to condone censorship, and by censorship I don't refer to controversy surrounding the so-called erotic book. I would be in jail today if forty years ago I had been selling books that you will find now in any bookstore. Words and subject matter that were considered offensive in the past are now, of course, acceptable and expected. What I mean by censorship is the proscribing of ideas and beliefs. I well remember the furor when Houghton Mifflin published and we dared to carry Hitler's *Mein Kampf*. Certain groups threatened to boycott our stores and actually advocated physical violence to force us to remove this book from sale. We were also accused of being pro- or anti-Catholic for carrying certain books. If we carried Mary Baker Eddy's books we were advocating Christian Science; if we didn't carry them, we were prejudiced or were censoring her beliefs. The list was endless and I spent a lot of time explaining to customers that just because we were stocking a book didn't mean that we were supporting any cause and that as responsible booksellers we had the obligation to carry controversial books on many subjects to give the reader an opportunity to make up his own mind.

To return to censorship as in "X-rated," a story, probably apocryphal, has always amused me. One noon Charles Scribner wished to speak to his noted editor Max Perkins and finding Perkins' office empty and his secretary away from her desk he looked at the editor's desk pad to see where he might be. He found the notations "Noon-lunch with Hemingway, 2 p.m.-four-letter word that denotes sexual intercourse (which I still can't bring myself to use casually). Incensed that his editor was evidently planning an assignation on company time, he later confronted Perkins and asked him about his memo. Max casually replied that he had lunch with Hemingway and later at the office tried to persuade him to delete the offending word from his forthcoming book. How times have changed!

What should be the relationship between bookseller and author? It is a many-faceted one. The bookseller must advise the young author, encourage the discouraged author, placate the suspicious author, and be friendly with the successful author. I feel that I helped a discouraged author when I wrote a "Tending Store" column about Harry Mark Petrakis and his book *Pericles on 31st Street*. Here is his reply:

April 14, 1965

Dear Mr. Kroch:
I was much moved by your warm and gracious reference to me and to my work in your column last Sunday. The words were strong and unqualified and your faith in my future is gratifying. I think it is true that all of us live under the dreadful burden of uncertainty. We can chart the course of a fatal illness from the moment of its inception to the moment when it kills us or someone close to us. The times in which we have these burdens are fierce and produce in many writers a kind of savage nihilism. It is not enough to obscure this despair with cliches and optimistic anticipations. We can only recognize that along with our responsibility to ourselves as writers, artists, we have a responsibility to others as well to try to render in compassionate and moving terms the human condition, the great unfathomable mystery of life and of men and women who weep and smile with one

face. When we are young we want all the radiant earth and no one can convince us that someday we will not have it. I think as we grow older we are willing to settle for much less. In my own experience I once wanted great fame and great wealth from my work. I would be grateful now for a little health, a little money, and the serenity of spirit to produce my books and stories. Even this achievement is a luxury which life does not always provide.

Thank you again. I did enjoy meeting you that afternoon in the store and look forward to a more leisurely visit sometime when we might talk.

Warmest best wishes,
Harry Mark Petrakis (signed)

Harry Mark Petrakis
2463 East 74th Place
Chicago, IL 60649

Harry and I have become fast friends and his books are enjoying the sale they so well deserve.

Theodore Dreiser was a suspicious author. He believed that his publishers were cheating him on royalties and he wrote representative booksellers asking them how many copies of a particular book of his they had sold. Dreiser believed that he could thus figure out how many books had been sold nationally and confront the publishers with what he thought were the actual sales figures and not the reported ones. He wrote my father about sales of *An American Tragedy* and

The 'Genius.' Dad answered him and here is Dreiser's reply:

June 3rd, 1929

My Dear Mr. Kroch:

Thank you very much for your letter in response to my request for information regarding sales of the *Genius* and the *Tragedy*. The figures you give are very helpful in my plan of comparison, and your high opinion of *Tragedy* is indeed a pleasurable one for me to hear.

Yours sincerely,
Theodore Dreiser (signed)
Box 202
General Post Office
New York City

Sinclair Lewis was a grateful author. In Dad's first edition of *Main Street* he wrote: "To Adolph Kroch, who has been one of the best friends of this book, with the greetings of Sinclair Lewis. Chicago, March 10, 1921.

Now for the author who needs deflating. A rather prominent one spent half an hour telling Dad how difficult it was to write a book, how much knowledge was required, how much study, and so on. Dad finally interrupted him and agreed with all the statements the author had made and said that he realized what brilliance it took to write a book. The Dad added, "But it takes a genius to sell one."

Good relationships with publishers are vital to any successful bookseller.

They can be most helpful to either a struggling young bookseller or an established one. I have been proud of my relationships with publishers. We have always wanted our share of any special incentives that are offered, such as co-op advertising, author appearances, or other promotional help, but we have never tried to take advantage of our good relationships. Booksellers and publishers need not be natural enemies. Both will prosper by working together.

The publisher I feel had the greatest impact on my business career was Richard L. Simon, cofounder of Simon & Schuster. Dick was the most innovative publisher I have every known. He had a tremendous influence in the entire industry. It was he who experimented, so successfully, with the odd price for books. He reasoned that when you went into a drugstore and bought a tube of toothpaste for seventy-nine cents you felt that it was marked down from a dollar and that you were getting bargain. Why not do the same thing with books? So he priced his books at $4.95, $7.95 and $14.95. I don't have to tell you that this is now a standard practice in the industry.

Simon & Schuster was one of the first publishers to use coupon advertising with the orders directed to them and not to dealers. Booksellers were incensed; S&S was stealing sales from them and they wouldn't sell their books. But that wasn't Dick's idea. He was merely creating a demand, which meant more sales for booksellers. And

that theory has been proven true.

Dick made two suggestions to me that I believe have been most useful. He said that the public generally is afraid to go into bookstores. They fear that some salesperson will correct their pronunciation of an author's name or that they, the customers, will show some degree of ignorance and embarrass themselves. Dick said, "Make people want to come into your store, make them feel at ease and welcome." I have tried to make the Kroch's & Brentano's stores pleasant places in which to shop. I stress that point to our sales staff continuously. No salesperson can know everything, but everyone can try to find the information the customer wants and make him or her feel welcome. Then, and only then, will a customer want to return to your store. Dick also urged that we advertise consistently. Not every ad will pay out but the cumulative result will be a recognition of your store as the place to buy books. We have advertized consistently in print, by direct mail, and on the radio for forty years, and it has paid off.

I believe a number of changes in the publisher-bookseller relationship must take place if the smaller independent bookseller is to prosper and perhaps even continue to exist. These are merely suggestions and are not necessarily my recommendations as some of them are not in the best interests of my firm. However, I feel they are worthy of consideration and study.

The first, and probably most revolutionary, is that books be sold on an outright, not a returnable basis. Discounts would have to be adjusted to enable the bookseller to absorb the cost of unsold books. However, disposing of these books would enable the bookseller to have an honest clearance sale which would attract customers to his store.

Books should be supplied to the retailer transportation paid. The cost of transportation should be reflected in the retail price of each book. Mass market paperback publishers already provide free transportation and evidently include this cost in the retail price. I believe such a change might require adjustments in the royalty agreements with authors, but I have been led to believe that many authors, and even the Authors Guild, are in favor of such a change. They believe it will be helpful, in particular, to the smaller independent bookseller who is able and anxious to do more for the budding young author than the chain operators.

The practice of giving a discount on the total purchase of a chain with shipment to each individual store should be eliminated. This so-called "drop shipping" is unfair and unjustified by any alleged savings. The cost of shipping, invoicing, and then probably processing returns from several hundred branches of a chain is certainly more expensive than a single transaction. For example, a smaller retailer who orders twenty-five copies of a book may receive a discount of 40 percent while his nearby competitor, a branch of a chain, could receive as

high as 48 percent for his order of twenty-five copies since this order was combined with the other branches of the chain.

All of the members of the book industry—publishers, booksellers, printers, yes, even authors—should make an agreed upon percentage of their gross receipts available for a national advertising campaign to encourage Americans to read. Other industries have launched this type of campaign with excellent results. Most people have heard and reacted to the "Say it with flowers" theme, for example. If we could instill an appetite for reading in today's nonreaders, the benefits would spread beyond the industry to the society at large.

These suggestions are controversial and I can only hope that they cause some publishers to reconsider their present relationship with their bookseller-customers.

In closing I believe a quotation from Jeremy Collier, written in 1698, is appropriate: Books are a guide in youth and an entertainment for age. They support us under solitude and prevent us from becoming a burden to ourselves. They help us to forget the crossness of men and things, compose our cares and passions, and lay our disappointments asleep.

I hold with Charles Lamb,
a wise bookseller
does more for the community
than all the lecturers, journalists,
and schoolmasters
put together.

John Cowper Powys
1872-1963

Colophon

Design: Ligature, Inc., Chicago, IL.
Pages composed on Apple® Macintosh
desktop publishing system using
Aldus® Pagemaker 3.0 software. Final
camera copy from Linotronic® 300.

Typography: Palatino Regular and
Bold, Roman and Italic.

Paper: Mohawk Superfine Cover Basis
80, Softwhite regular finish. Mohawk
Superfine, Text Basis 80, White
smooth finish.

Printing and binding: Bookcrafters,
Chelsea, MI.